Oppos... selecti...

Harawira's lawyer gets elected to rust board

Traffic officers object to Maori courses

Maori Claims 'Threat To Electricity'

'KILL A WHITE'

and

Maori activist group inflames gathering on university marae

Maori fishing settlement overrides rule of law

Activists Speed Pakeha Exodus To Queensland

AND CRIME: URE OF FEAR

Gangs 'shock troops in land issue'

...e riots 'likely ...ext 10 years'

Book attacking Maori beliefs not racist, say police

...aori Claim Covers ...arge Area of Bay

BETWEEN THE LINES

Cover painting: 'Mo Irihapeti Tenei Karanga' by Robyn Kahukiwa, 1988.
Alkyd oil, paper collage and oil diptych on canvas. 1988 mm × 2635 mm.
Produced for the exhibition Whakamamae (2 April–19 June 1988) at Wellington City Art Gallery. Collection Irihapeti Ramsden. Photography by John Casey, courtesy Wellington City Art Gallery.

'Mo Irihapeti Tenei Karanga' belongs to a series of paintings and pastel drawings conceived as a protest against the colonisation of the karanga by Pakeha women. Shocked by the intrusion of Pakeha women into the tapu of the karanga, Irihapeti Ramsden shared her anger and grief with her friend Robyn Kahukiwa. Robyn's response was the protest series.

Many Maori women see the colonisation of the karanga as a breach of Article II of the Treaty of Waitangi — indeed, as an extension of Pakeha colonisation in general. This breach of the Treaty is symbolised by the torn copies of the Treaty on the amo and the maihi of the house. The call of Maori women supported by their tipuna clears the wairua pathway for the gathering of the living.

*Much love &
good reading*

*Geoff
May 1990*

BETWEEN THE LINES

Racism and the
New Zealand Media

Edited by
PAUL SPOONLEY
and
WALTER HIRSH

HEINEMANN REED

Editors' note

A notable and regrettable omission from this collection is an analysis of the 'kill a white' incident at the University of Auckland marae, since media treatment of this affair exemplifies many of the concerns expressed in this book about the reporting of race relations issues. Wasi Shortland, for 10 years a Maori Community Officer with the Department of Maori Affairs and now a journalist with *Te Karere*, attended the marae meeting and subsequently wrote a point-by-point critique of the original *Sunday Star* 'exposé' for inclusion in this book. At the time of writing, the *Star* story remains the subject of an Equal Opportunities Tribunal hearing. It was the unanimous view of the legal experts we approached that a public discussion of the reporting of the affair would be unlikely to prejudice the Tribunal hearing. Despite this the editor of the *Star* chose to deny us the opportunity to reproduce the offending story, which effectively made a specific critique impracticable. Was it in the public interest to suppress open debate of this controversial affair? We think not. In any case, we take this opportunity to thank Wasi Shortland for his work and apologise for its exclusion from the present collection.

Published by Heinemann Reed, a division of Octopus Publishing Group (NZ) Ltd,
39 Rawene Road, Birkenhead, Auckland.
Associated companies, branches and representatives throughout the world.

ISBN 0 7900 0119 5

First published 1990

Designed by Richard King
Typeset by Typocrafters Ltd, Auckland
Printed in Singapore

Contents

I
The Media and Race Relations

II
The Medium and the Message

III
Case Studies

IV
Directions

Acknowledgements

The editors would like to acknowledge the very important contribution made to this book by various people and organisations. The staff of the Race Relations Office have been supportive; Heni Johnson, Maleni Tavilione, Laina Kinkaid and Kate Clementson have helped the book's progress by their valuable work. Members of the Department of Sociology, Massey University, have also contributed to making the book a reality.

Other people provided guidance and help as the book developed: Gary Wilson's inside knowledge of the media and his advice on key matters have played an important role; and Andrew Campbell and Jem Bates of Heinemann Reed provided a critical sounding board at various stages. In particular, we really appreciate Jem's commitment to the book and the long hours he spent in seeing the book through to its completion. Tony McCracken helped with the onerous task of proofreading.

Finally, we would like to thank the hosts and participants at the race relations and media hui held at Te Herenga Waka Marae in 1988. The concern and anger expressed on that occasion helped crystallise the issues for us and provided an important incentive. This book is as much theirs as it is ours.

Introduction

This book reflects our concern, and that of others, about the way in which the media report race relations in New Zealand. It is meant not as a 'media bashing' exercise but rather as a contribution towards improving standards within the media and, thereby, the quality of communication and debate, which is crucial to the improvement of intergroup relations. To this end, the book contains a collection of diverse viewpoints. What constitutes a problem, and what ought to be done about it, varies considerably according to the contributor. But all are agreed that there is an urgent need for the media to improve their performance and to play a more constructive role in reporting on, and influencing, New Zealand's race relations.

The need for such an improvement was highlighted during 1987 and 1988 when the media coverage of certain incidents, notably the Maori Loans Affair and the so-called 'kill a white' incident, encouraged a moral panic amongst Pakeha. Maori issues and views were misrepresented by the media. Pakeha and other ethnic groups were encouraged to see Maori as a threat in a variety of ways. The selective reporting of the issues and the resultant curtailed public debate reinforced our concern about the media's handling of race relations. Of course, these two events are by no means the only ones which have raised doubts about the media's performance. The last few years have been punctuated by a series of media-determined incidents. Some are highlighted in this book.

The next matter of concern was the apparent unwillingness of sections of the media to subject themselves to the same critical scrutiny that they practised on others. Admittedly, some in the media welcomed the debate, and a number of these individuals are represented in this book, but others responded defensively or were simply apathetic. The media exercise enormous power in an information-oriented and technologically sophisticated society such as ours. When questions are raised about the exercise of that power, many in the media seem quite prepared to defend the status quo despite the need to reflect the very different conditions which prevail in the 1990s. When minority groups have asked to exercise their right of reply or, increasingly, for the right to offer alternative information and entertainment services, they have run up against opposition, hostility or indifference. So the inaccuracies of mainstream media coverage have been compounded by the problems of establishing alternative sources of information and the media's reluctance to accept responsibility for the shortfalls in media services.

These issues raise fundamental questions about intergroup relations and the distribution of power in New Zealand. Historically, the media have played an important and highly questionable role in the process of colonisation as they have convinced coloniser and colonised that what was occurring was in the interests of both. This media monoculturalism persists, and the challenges of biculturalism, and undoubtedly cultural pluralism in the future, inevitably lead to questions about the ownership and control of the media.

New forms of state ownership of the media as well as a growing commercial and private influence have encouraged many to take a greater interest in the media services they get. Minority interests (Maori and others) are poorly catered for. If influence over policy is minimal, then the issue becomes one of ownership. After all, who decides what is 'fair' in terms of participation and representation in the media? How should Maori culture and practice be incorporated into what the media do? And would not Maori interests be better served by services which they either owned or had significant control over?

The present book airs these concerns. A variety of people inside the media, and some outside it, were approached to offer their opinions or to report on their experiences. An important event in the process of organising this book was the hui on race relations and the media at Te Herenga Waka Marae, Victoria University of Wellington, which took place in September 1988. Organised jointly by the whanau of the marae and the Race Relations Office, the hui brought together many who felt strongly about the media's role in contemporary race relations. Significantly, some of those who should have been there to listen to the debates were not. But the anger expressed and experiences shared on the marae confirmed the need for wider public debate. Many of those who attended the hui have contributed chapters to this book. Others who it was hoped would participate in the project, particularly a number of concerned women, were unfortunately unable to because of pressure of work.

All contributors are critical of the media's role in contemporary race relations — those working inside the media as much so as those who are on the 'receiving end' of media coverage. It is in the area of solutions that differences become marked. Some argue that journalists' training ought to be more culturally sensitive. Others see policy matters such as local and culturally balanced television programming as central issues. Others see no option but separate media networks and services for Maori and other ethnic minority communities. For the latter, the present system has been found wanting to the extent that no amount of tinkering could counter its major inadequacies.

Fundamental to these debates and the exploration of various options is the importance of the media in defining public understanding and opinion. When direct experience is not possible (and at times, even when it is), the media become the principal means by which we understand what is happening in our community, playing a major role in identifying what is a problem, and what is not.

Information provided via the media will reinforce or challenge the views held by one group about another. If 'overstaying' is considered by the public to be a problem, it will be because it is represented as such by the media. If Pacific Islanders are defined as the overstayers — quite inaccurately — then again, the media will have provided the 'information' which underlies this public perception. So the media supply us with information about ourselves and our community. For very many people, they are the *only* source of information and become a substitute for direct experience.

In addition to providing information and entertainment, the media are also critical to the success or otherwise of democratic debate. The way in which the media treat minority issues strongly influences whether those issues are taken seriously in the public arena. Further, if basic information is missing, the majority may overrule minority interests based on incomplete or inaccurate information. Participation in the political process by Maori and other minority ethnic groups will be influenced by their access to the media and the extent to which their views are adequately represented. The media are critical to the success of the democratic system. If the range of opinion is not fairly represented in the media's presentation of issues, then democracy can be said to have been denied to one group or another. For this and other reasons, the role of the media will become more important in the next decade. The power to exercise influence through the media will determine success in many other areas.

Finally, while it is our aim to raise questions about the media in this country, we should indicate in passing that the way in which New Zealand's race relations are portrayed by the international media is also a matter of concern. Many of the reports appearing overseas have been alarmist in predicting a 'racial revolution' of one sort or another. As we have already indicated, this book is intended to provide a critical review of the media's performance in this country. But it is worth noting that the international media need to be subjected to the same scrutiny, and that our experiences of how the media cover New Zealand stories might hold lessons for us about the way in which many world events and overseas issues are covered. If we are going to exercise critical judgement with regard to the New Zealand media, then we should not suspend that critical stance when it comes to reports from or about other countries.

Walter Hirsh
Paul Spoonley
July 1989

I

THE MEDIA
&
RACE RELATIONS

IN THIS SECTION, five writers explore the relationship between the media and race relations in New Zealand. These chapters are a general introduction to the issues.

First, Steve Maharey provides an understanding of the media in New Zealand and describes the values and practices which prevail. He invites the reader to take a critical look at the media but cautions against assuming a simple cause and effect relationship between the media and public attitudes. Paul Spoonley reinforces these points and makes a direct connection between the media's role and the changing nature of local race relations. What is the media's contribution to public debate and knowledge? Is it a positive or negative contribution? Ranginui Walker begins with a potted history of Maori–Pakeha relations, before discussing the way in which the media have misconstrued Maori concerns to a Pakeha audience.

Gary Wilson examines the competence of journalists and media management in the area of race relations, and argues that a woeful ignorance of New Zealand history and Maori experience prevails. He challenges journalists to address the issue of media incompetence and racism, and to do something about it. Bernard Kernot ends this opening section with a discussion of race-tagging, the practice of identifying a person by a racial label even where this information is quite irrelevant to the story. The effect is to reinforce negative images of minorities: race-tagging is frequently evident in the reporting of criminal offending, for example.

The media have the potential to play a positive role in our race relations. Those who work in the media can improve understanding and decrease tension simply by doing their jobs more professionally. The commentators in this section all argue that the media, for the moment, have not begun to realise this potential.

Chapter 1
UNDERSTANDING THE MASS MEDIA
Steve Maharey

Every one of us, each day, in New Zealand is touched by the media. Newspapers, radio, film, television and advertising surround us. They are pervasive, impinging on our daily routines, our daily lives, communicating, influencing, affecting, determining.[1]

It is now a cliché to say that New Zealanders live in a media-saturated society. For those who can spare the time there are, on an annual basis, 10 490 hours of television to watch, 82 radio stations to listen to and 33 daily newspapers plus 590 magazines, journals and newsletters to read.[2] Now television can offer TV3, soon to be followed by direct satellite broadcasts bringing numerous other channels. From the alarm which switches on the bedside radio, and advertising at the indoor cricket complex, to magazines on the coffee table and home videos, our lives are pervaded by the media. The question is: does it matter?

The answer must be that it does, because the media help us 'not simply to know more about "the world", but to make sense of it'.[3] To make sense of the world, the media must represent the world to us in particular ways. They must choose who we will hear about, what and who should be left unnoticed, and how things, people, events and relationships should be represented. This power to define the world is what makes the media crucial to an understanding of contemporary race relations in New Zealand.

The effect of the media

For many people, the power of the media is not in doubt. Politicians, for example, clearly believe that the media, particularly television, have become crucial in winning or losing elections, as was well illustrated during the 1987 election campaign in which political activities were carefully geared to the needs of the media.

> This month, as another general election approaches, the politicians and their image-makers and strategists are once more out to win voters' hearts and minds.
>
> Millions have been spent in the cause of mass persuasion as voters are targeted and bombarded with research policies and professional packaging. Campaigns full of showbiz and razzmatazz have been carefully structured around the Leader and the 6.30 News.
>
> This is undoubtedly the most high pressure, image-conscious, television-oriented and professionally driven campaign New Zealanders have ever seen.[4]

In moving towards a strategy of fighting elections through the media, New Zealand politicians are following what are believed to be tried and true formulae used overseas, particularly in the United States. There are disputes about the relative effectiveness of the millions spent on media budgets, but no one is prepared to take the risk and remain with the old style of politics.

People are apt to become cynical when they read of huge advertising budgets and politicians competing for evening news. Yet it seems that most people have come to associate the media with the power to influence behaviour. Conservatives blame the media for a decline in morals and a rise in violence. They seek strong censorship to ensure the young are not exposed to the 'wrong' messages. With equal fervour, radicals see the media as the avenue through which those who hold power in New Zealand, as employers, or because they are white, male or heterosexual, maintain their positions and oppress others.

The question of what effect the media have may, of course, be settled by turning to social scientists for advice. But the answers are not as clear cut as the prevailing commonsense assumptions about the role of the media would suggest.

An understanding of the mass media

Interest in the mass media among social scientists can be traced back to a group of academics, known as the Frankfurt School, working in Germany during the 1930s as the Nazis were coming to power. The Frankfurt School observed that the Nazis were very enthusiastic about the power of radio and film to indoctrinate the masses. They became convinced that the way the media were being used offered new and worrying possibilities for control. However, they did not confine their concerns to media use by the Nazis. Because of their dissident views, most members of the Frankfurt School had to flee Germany as the Nazis established their power. Many of them went to the United States, where they perceived the same use of the media, albeit in the service of selling products rather than totalitarianism.

A striking confirmation of the Frankfurt School's views on media influence was offered in New York in 1939. Orson Welles' adaptation of the H. G. Wells story *War of the Worlds* used the device of a fake news bulletin to announce a Martian invasion. Soon after the start of the programme, thousands of listeners crowded the roads in a panic attempt to escape from the city.[5]

A similar event occurred in New Zealand 10 years later.

> The wasps are coming! The wasps are coming!
> The cry might have been heard in any Auckland suburb on the morning of 1 April 1949. Phil Shone, the 1ZB breakfast session announcer, had just put over a special bulletin. 'A swarm of wasps has been sighted moving east of Papatoetoe. It's reported to be one mile wide and several hundred yards deep, and it's being kept under observation to give fair warning of the direction it takes as it approaches Auckland city.'
> . . . Housewives dutifully heeded advice on anti-wasp precautions. Smear jam or honey on bits of paper and leave them outside the door. Close all doors. Wear protective clothing. Excitement and apprehension were intense.[6]

It was, as the listeners discovered with a mixture of relief and annoyance, an April Fool's Day joke.

Despite apparently clear demonstrations that the media could directly influence what people thought and did, social scientists in the United States remained unconvinced. In part, this can be attributed to the different cultural values of Americans. People who think of themselves as free individuals are unlikely to readily accept that they are at the mercy of the media. Instead of endorsing the Frankfurt School's claims, many of which had been readily accepted by advertisers and the public at large, social scientists condemned them. To prove their point, they began studying the direct effects of the media's output, looking at such things as the influence of party political broadcasts on voting behaviour, of marketing campaigns on consumer intentions, and whether children shown violent films felt driven to copy what they saw.

Much to the chagrin of those who saw the media as all-powerful, the most consistent conclusion to emerge was that there are very few examples of the media's having a direct effect. These results reflected the fact that most people forget almost everything they have seen as soon as a programme is finished, or remember it only selectively. If the media have an effect, they concluded, it is not direct, like an injection from a hypodermic needle. What influence there is must be much more subtle.

To study this more subtle effect, social scientists made use of their knowledge of how American society actually worked. They pointed to the important role of the social group — friends, neighbours and respected opinion makers — through which, they argued, media messages had to be filtered. These social groups stand between the individual and the media. Summarising this American research, most of which took place during the 1950s and 1960s, one leading academic wrote: 'Mass communication does not ordinarily serve as a necessary and sufficient cause of audience effects, but rather functions through a number of mediating factors.'[7] In other words, the scope of media influence was thought to be largely limited to reinforcing and reproducing what people already think and do.

Another important research finding, which has added support to the view that the media have a limited effect, suggested that members of an audience differ greatly in the way they react to the same television programme. While it may impress some, others will reject it, switch it off or ignore it and do something else. Leading on from these points, studies of the *uses* and *gratifications* which people get from the various media underline both the wide differences in audience response and the deep need many people have for the media. For example, radio listeners have described how radio takes their mind off other things; is like a friend calling in; helps keep them cheerful; keeps their mind active; helps keep them going; and keeps them involved with life. In a sentence, the general consensus was that 'it's not so much what the media do with people but what people do with the media'.[8]

These American findings contain many truths that should give pause when considering the role of the media in race relations. In the midst of a bitter argument over racism, it is easy to find the media guilty of producing the problem. However, it has to be acknowledged that there are other influences on people's lives which come between them and a media item. In the case of the Orson Welles broadcast, we can point to the Cold War climate of opinion in America as more to blame than the broadcast itself. Further, we can see that while the media may be pervasive, people interact with programmes in very different ways, according to their personal circumstances and needs in relation to the media.

But there are weaknesses in the above conclusions which more recent research has tried to correct. The work continued because it seemed to many people that the findings of the mainly American researchers implied we could safely ignore the media, yet this conclusion appeared to fly in the face of the growing influence of the media. It was argued that the media must have some effect on their audiences if only because people were spending more and more time interacting with them. Once again, the Americans took the lead. The central theme of the findings for the National Commission on Causes and Prevention of Violence, reporting in 1972, was that television must have some effect on audiences; if it sells products, it must also influence behaviour. The question remained as to how this influence was exerted.

The answers were to come this time from across the Atlantic, from British and European researchers who suggested that previous research had been limited by focusing on the question of direct effects. Perhaps the most significant conclusion that emerged was that the effect of the media does not result from individual programmes or advertisements or news items at all. Rather, it results from the overall role of the mass media, which is to select and provide social knowledge. In a modern society, people live fragmented and divided lives. They live within narrow boundaries, within a series of private spheres, forcing a reliance on the media for knowledge about the rest of society. The media provide and select images about other people, and it is through the media that a picture of the overall society can be gained.

In opposition to the American findings, these conclusions suggest that in modern societies the role of groups in filtering and influencing the media's information to the individual is breaking down. What used to happen in pubs, at sports matches, in community halls and at other social occasions now occurs largely in domestic situations. More than face to face experience, or any other social institution (including schools), it is the media which entertain and inform. They 'define reality' and 'set agendas': they decide what the important issues of the day are, who should be listened to and who should be marginalised, ignored, ridiculed and stereotyped. Further, the agenda the media construct is overwhelmingly oriented towards the status quo view of the world.[9]

In comparison with the earlier American conclusions, more recent work on the mass media has concluded that they have an increasingly important role. This conclusion does not mean that we can now return to the old ideas that the effects are direct and easily measurable. Rather, in the context of the way we live in modern societies, we can say that, taken together, the media have become the key means by which the world is represented to us. The power of the media is exercised by representing the world and world events to us in certain definite ways.

Learning about the mass media

Upon hearing that the mass media exercise real power, some people may feel there is a case for strong censorship and control. But perhaps the more appropriate response is to ensure that people understand how the process of *representation* actually works.

The best place to begin is with a concrete example.[10] Look at the picture below. What do you see?

Photo: Gil Hanly

A Maori youth? No, it is not a Maori youth, it is a *picture* of a Maori youth. This may seem a subtle distinction, but it allows us to take our first step towards understanding representation. We have to realise that even news journalism, with its emphasis on 'getting the facts', does not simply deliver the world to us in unprocessed lumps through television, radio or newspapers. *All* mass media work by using language — words, text, pictures (still or moving). These are combined in different ways through the practices and techniques of selection, editing, montage, design, layout, format, linkage, narrative, openings and closures to represent the world to us. Some of these ways may be 'factual', some 'investigative', some 'fictional', some merely 'entertaining'. They all work and can only work because they are able to construct the world for us in a meaningful way.[11]

What the media produce can best be understood using the concept *text*. By text is meant the film, the newspaper photo, the magazine advertisement, the song on the radio — anything which the media have put together to get a message across. We are used to thinking of books as texts because we have been taught to understand books, fiction or non-fiction, as having been produced by authors. This same understanding now has to be applied to all media. Just as books have to be written using particular conventions (such as correct grammar), a television programme has to use various rules or *codes* if it is to make sense to its audience. This is easily illustrated. Think about the way television programmes are introduced: images appear on the screen; music is heard; the images change as one shot is exchanged for another; particular colours dominate. As the programme is introduced we, the viewers, can quickly recognise the usual introductory ingredients of an adventure tale, a news broadcast or a comedy show. Blurred images, loud, fast music, one image quickly exchanged for another and blue colour tonings usually herald a crime programme. The skilful synthesis of all the elements of a television programme according to rules and codes allows meaning to be conveyed.

Those who work in the media make use, consciously or unconsciously, of established codes to produce what we then read, see or hear. They not only publish material about the world, they also construct it. This is not just a technical process, because it also involves making assumptions, often unconscious, about the best way to present a message. As media professionals put together the elements of a message, they create what social scientists call *discourse* — a particular way of representing reality. Let's take a particular use of words as an illustration. Besides having a literal meaning, a denotation, words also have an implied meaning, a connotation. The selective use of the words 'girl' and 'woman' have provoked controversy in the area of sports broadcasting for many years because of the broadcasters' persistence in referring to female athletes as 'girls'. Many people have complained that it is demeaning to refer to adult females as girls because it suggests that they are immature and not to be taken seriously. It is pointed out that, in contrast, adult male athletes are always referred to as men rather than boys. For some, this may seem a trivial issue, but in the context of wider efforts by women to gain recognition in a world constructed largely around the interests of men, it has considerable significance. In choosing the word 'girl' rather than 'woman', a broadcaster draws upon a specific set of attitudes and conventions, thereby helping to construct and represent the world in a particular way.

These concepts of text, codes and discourse help us to understand how the mass media construct the view of the world we the audience receive. Contrary to some opinion, the media do not provide a 'window on the world'. It is important to stress that this is the case whether we are discussing the news or a soap opera. From the opening sequence to the closing credits, the news is a particular conceptualisation of the day's events. In their work on New Zealand television news and current affairs, Loader and Bosshard[12] make the point that media professionals work hard to make their selective construction of the day's events look real and true. The presenters talk straight to the camera, read their lines from an autocue, and wear middle-of-the-road style clothes. They use phrases like 'many New Zealanders think' when introducing a question in order to give the impression that what they ask is of concern to everyone, despite the fact that they seldom have any way of knowing what people in general think. An authoritative tone of voice is required of newsreaders, and those who do not measure up are removed.[13] And, perhaps most importantly, television takes us to the scene to see for ourselves what is happening.

It is vital that people become familiar with the way in which news and current affairs make what is a highly selective and constructed view of the world look real. This is not to say that our news and current affairs programmes simply do not tell the truth. Rather, we as viewers need to be sophisticated in critically analysing the version of events we are being presented with so that we recognise it as just that — a *version* of events.

Loader and Bosshard's work may come as a surprise to people who regard the news as simply a presentation of the facts. Indeed, it is the appearance of being factual that makes the news so *ideologically* powerful. Ideology is a very important but difficult concept. For present purposes, we will define it as 'the ways in which meaning serves to sustain relations of domination' in a society.[14] In the production of ideas, images, routines and practices, the media shape our view of the world in particular ways. To take an example, the media, in choosing to talk about issues of race and ethnic relations, have to decide how to present events. The Maori nationalist argument is different from the racist argument which is different from the liberal argument. The media have some choices to make, but being guided by principles of 'neutrality, impartiality and balance', they are likely to look for 'a range of views' while anchoring discussion to what they perceive to be the most acceptable view. The majority view is the one to take. But in doing this, the media reinforce a particular worldview and marginalise other views. In recent times, the media have been made to realise just how tenuous this hold on 'reality' is by challenges from Maori spokespeople as to how they are represented, or ignored, by the media.[15]

Does this mean we should adopt a posture of total distrust of the media? No. What is needed is open and informed debate about how the media construct our view of the world. Because it is impossible for the media to bring everything that happens to our living rooms, selection and construction will always be part of the way the media operate. The more this process is out in the open, the more it can be debated and the media forced to reflect the diversity of interests within New Zealand.

Media organisations

If the media do influence how people think and behave, then the matter of who is in control becomes very important. In terms of overall structure, New Zealand presently has what might be called a mixed economy of the media. However, this mix of ownership has not prevented a drastic concentration of control in a few hands. Two newspaper companies, Independent News Limited and Wilson and Horton, totally dominate New Zealand's daily newspaper production. The state controls two television channels and 64 radio stations. There are 22 privately owned radio stations and one private television channel. However, as with newspapers, ownership is concentrated in the hands of a few companies. In addition, there is a trend by companies involved in the media towards owning a mix of newspapers, radio stations and magazines and seeking a stake in the television market.

Such concentration of ownership, either in the hands of the state or in private ownership, raises questions about direct censorship and control over what is produced. However, the record shows that apart from the early days of the press, it has been rare for owners to direct what is produced; that is not to say that direction has been absent, and there have been some notorious examples. In 1972, the editor of the *Listener*, Alexander Macleod, as a result of a clearly political decision, was dismissed for writing what were considered by the New Zealand Broadcasting Corporation Board to be unsuitable editorials on critical issues of the day.

The possibility of direct interference is enough to make it imperative that ownership and control are the subject of constant public scrutiny. Yet by far the most important control is not very sensational. As one commentator stated in relation to the privately owned press, 'Editors work for the Establishment by instinct and training, not by management from outside.'[16]

While it has become fashionable for newspapers, radio talkback and some television current affairs programmes to be more critical (or perhaps sensational) in recent years, there is no doubt that the New Zealand media, for the most part, remain very close to the middle ground in everything. Control over the media is less a case of being told what to do by an elite than the way quite routine and often unconscious factors shape the products of media organisations. Some of these factors are outlined below.

Recruitment

We can begin by considering who works for media organisations. As a general rule, the people hired are just like the people already there. In practice, this means that the people who are often marginalised in programmes, such as Maori and Pacific Islanders, are also barely represented in the organisation that produces the programmes. The results of this pattern of recruitment are overwhelmingly obvious.

In response to a request by the Royal Commission on Social Policy for the figures on Maori staff, Television New Zealand estimated that about 56 out of 1860 employees (3 percent) were Maori. It further estimated that perhaps one-third of that 56 were fluent speakers of Maori. Radio New Zealand was unable to say with certainty how many Maori staff it had, but estimated 50 out of a total of 1 200 (4 percent) were Maori.[17]

This situation is improving as both Television New Zealand and Radio New Zealand have set themselves new recruitment targets. Yet improvements will remain difficult to implement while those already in the job do not themselves think it vitally important to recruit people from different backgrounds from their own.

Professional ideology

One of the main reasons media professionals cannot understand the problems highlighted by recruitment practices is that they tend to share a particular view of the media. This view has been well put by Gary Wilson, executive officer for the New Zealand Journalists' Training Board.

> Journalists often argue that their job is simply to hold a mirror up to society so the public can see what is really going on. It is a comforting analogy for journalists because it relieves them of a moral dilemma. If they are criticised for covering a story, they have a convenient defence: they are just doing their job.

They are not making judgements, they say; they are not taking sides. They are merely delivering an objective, professional summary to keep the public informed.[18]

With this understanding of the nature of the media it does not really matter who puts the news together, chooses television programmes or writes radio plays. Since the media professional is just reflecting what society does and wants, there can be no problem. This belief is, of course, nonsense, but its currency means any debate about the way the media represent society needs to go on inside as well as outside media organisations. Media professionals need to become aware of how they and their institutions work so they might then become committed to a process of change.

Gatekeepers

Because those in the media get to choose what does and does not get into print, on radio or television, they have become recognised as *gatekeepers*. They decide what will be talked about on the news, what the emphasis of this season's crop of television comedies will be and what faces will appear in a commercial. In the area of news, this can be particularly important, reflecting the values that journalists and editors have through their perception of events. Research shows that 'newsworthiness' is judged according to the following general criteria:[19]

Simplicity
An event must be important to qualify as news, yet relatively unambiguous in its meaning. Problematic and complex issues are difficult for a newspaper to deal with and impractical for the visually dependent medium of television. Keeping things simple also means that news will usually be about something with which audiences are already familiar.

A single viewing of the early evening television news will clearly demonstrate the demand for simplicity. During a half-hour broadcast, complex issues are reduced to very brief items within a format which seeks to give viewers an authoritative account of the 'day's events'.

Drama
Newsworthiness also depends on recognising how an event can be visualised as important or as indicating a dramatic development. Obviously what is considered dramatic will depend on what else is available, who is involved, familiarity with the issues and a host of other elements. A very large and important gathering among Pacific Islanders may, on these grounds, be ignored because the Pakeha journalist has no way of understanding its significance.

Personal relevance
Events are usually portrayed in terms of the key individuals involved and the effects on individuals of what has transpired. Whatever public figures do tends to make the news. Items which can be related directly to people's experience, such as the story of a small child lost in the bush, are ideal material.

Themes and continuity
A particular event is more newsworthy if it is contiguous with previous events,

so that a reporter is able to place it within a familiar framework. This means that news is often not new. Rather, reporters recognise events as stories because they fit with common themes. A possible story about Mongrel Mob members visiting a marae may be bypassed in favour of a retailer's complaint that gang members congregated outside his or her shop.

Consonance

Often events are prejudged in the sense that a reporter will have a clear idea of what is wanted for a story to emerge. For example, a demonstration will be expected to yield some violence and possibly some arrests. If these do not happen, the event may not be regarded as news.

Surprise

While continuity and consonance are the stock-in-trade of news, the unexpected can always push through. Things that upset the normal expectations and have an effect (preferably negative) on people are likely to be made into news. Bad news is good news for the media.

Accommodation

Finally, whether an event becomes news may depend on something as simple as whether it can be conveniently accommodated. During January, journalists are so desperate for news that they are likely to make a story of events they will totally ignore later in the year.

The examples of recruitment, professional ideology and gatekeeping show that the routines and rules that govern the media are themselves enough to ensure control is exercised. But it is necessary to note once again that despite the power of media professionals, the audience should not be seen as mere victims. Whatever message a programme or item intends to get across, there is no guarantee that everyone will take the same meaning. Indeed, it has now become accepted wisdom to talk about media messages as having a *preferred meaning* — the meaning intended by the producers. But audiences often 'read' messages in very different ways — some accepting, others rejecting or opposing. In an interesting English study, David Morley interviewed various social groups about their responses to the BBC current affairs programme *Nationwide*.[20] Those accepting the preferred reading included bank managers and apprentices; those rejecting *Nationwide* included black further education students and shop stewards. In between were teacher training and university students and trade union officials who negotiated a meaning.

These findings suggest that a programme which is intended to portray the superior values of one group may actually be understood (or read) in a quite different way. And the more audiences are aware of the selective construction they are being offered by the media, the more different readings are likely to occur. There is further work to be done in this area, but it needs to be kept in mind that audiences are active in their response to the media.

Reforming the media

In recent years, a growing awareness of the role of the media in society has led to a variety of groups seeking reform. This is vitally important work because in the midst of the so-called communications revolution it seems that the media are becoming less open to democratic control. What is causing this is the move towards commercialisation.

Ever since the beginning of broadcasting in New Zealand there has been an ongoing debate over whether television and radio should be privately or publicly owned. Until recently, it was assumed that public ownership was essential to ensure that the public interest was served. However, during the 1970s and 1980s there was a steady undermining of the public service tradition of broadcasting in favour of the private market. The argument has been that public service broadcasting is a monoply which does not give people what they want; letting private broadcasters on to the scene would ensure more variety, more choice and better service. The fact that a century of privately owned newspaper production has not resulted in this kind of service is seldom mentioned in the debate.

In the face of such criticism, New Zealand public service broadcasting has responded by acting more and more like a commercial enterprise. It has been pushed further in this direction since successive governments have limited the licence fee which supports state-owned television and radio. To make money, public service broadcasting has had to rely on commercial advertising and seek a mass audience for popular programmes. Many opportunities to experiment with different kinds of programming have been thwarted by the need to remain commercially viable.

With the election of the Labour Government in 1984, the debate about private versus publicly owned media came to a head. The Labour Government has shown such a strong preference for private ownership that even state-owned organisations have been forced to behave as if they were in the private sector. Public service goals have not been abandoned completely, but they have been displaced by commercial goals.

Does this matter? In a useful submission to the Royal Commission on Social Policy, Farnsworth argues that it does, and points out how overseas experience shows that market-oriented media perform badly when it comes to quality, equity and access. What begins as a promise of unlimited choice quickly fades as ownership of the media is concentrated into fewer hands, with an emphasis on profits derived from large markets. So the 'structure of media markets leads advertising to restrict the range and quality of programming possibilities. In addition, advertising, in tandem with consistent trends to conglomeration and concentration, deters new entrants to the market unless they already have resources.' In conclusion, Farnsworth argues that the 'free' market does not live up to expectations and needs to be regulated and given incentives to function in a socially equitable way.[21]

It should not be taken from this discussion, however, that we abandon reform and return to traditional public service broadcasting. An important reason for the move towards the private market is that the public service tradition was paternalistic and provided largely what the producers of the media decided people wanted. Thirty years of public service television has resulted in less than 1 percent of Maori language programmes being broadcast in 1987.[22] The failure to reflect the variety of cultural interests, attitudes and values within New Zealand society has been a real weakness of public service broadcasting. The future, then, belongs neither to the old public service model nor to the emerging private sector model. Rather, what is required is a shift towards a more democratic media whereby audiences and media professionals work together to ensure a truly diverse media.

It will not be easy to achieve such change in New Zealand given the trend towards commercialisation and private ownership of the media. To a large degree, what progress can be made will depend on clear terms of reference for an alternative view to be put forward. The following broad principles, drawn from the work of Golding and Murdoch, are identified here as conditions which would need to be met if New Zealand is to have a democratic media.[23]

Diversity
There are three parts to this. First, we must ensure that the widest possible range of information is in circulation. Secondly, we must ensure that an extensive range of viewpoints and interpretations is on offer. Thirdly, we must promote the widest possible range of media.

Accessibility
Accessibility means ensuring that no one is barred from the means to communicate publicly or to buy communications because of characteristics which they are powerless to influence. The aim is to maximise the range of experiences, both social and personal, that can be communicated while at the same time promoting access to the full range of the media. In particular, the aim should be to ensure that income, gender, ethnicity and location are not barriers to the full range of communication facilities.

Accountability
Accountability involves developing channels through which consumers and users of communications systems can have the opportunity to make their opinions, needs and demands felt, both at the level of day-to-day use and the level of overall policy direction.

These general goals for media reform will, of course, be extremely difficult to put into practice and we do not have the space to identify specific strategies here. As a general principle though, for reform to be possible a substantial proportion of the media must remain in public hands. This does not mean a return to the old style of state control. Rather the state needs to ensure that there is a regulated space within which a range of media activities can take place. Some activities may be provided directly by the state; some may be provided in partnership with particular groups; still others may involve private companies or individuals doing what they want. The state is vital to ensuring that possibilities for diverse, accessible and accountable media continue to exist and develop, but beyond that, its direct role should depend on whether it is the best agent to provide the services. Such a model offers tremendous advantages, if there is to be a more democratic media, over both the traditional public service and current private sector models.

Conclusion

The purpose of this chapter has been to explore the means by which the media make sense of the world. Through processes of selection and construction, the media represent the world in a particular and definite way. Audiences need not and do not necessarily accept what they are given, but in modern society they are increasingly reliant on the media for entertainment and information. It is the power to define reality and set the agenda of issues that makes the media of crucial importance to race relations in contemporary New Zealand society. What this chapter has suggested is that having understood how the media work, there is a need for people to seek reform so that a different, more democratic media might emerge to meet the interests of all New Zealanders.

Chapter 2

RACISM, RACE RELATIONS AND THE MEDIA

Paul Spoonley

> When legislation enacted in the name of equality visibly fails to defend your rights
> and yet is not seriously challenged in the news media you feel that those media
> must belong to someone else. When at a local level you know of blacks fighting
> against exploitation and harassment and see the press presenting a biased truth,
> a white truth, then you know to whom the media belong.[1]

An overstatement? It rather depends on who you ask. The above quotation describes
the situation in Britain in the 1970s, but it encompasses some of the universals
that are characteristic of the relationship between minority groups and the media
in all western countries. In line with the present book's critical focus on this
relationship in New Zealand, this chapter outlines *some* of the factors that contribute to a concern and at times a deep anger over the power of the media to
define events in their own terms. The material here serves to remind us, if anyone
needs reminding, that race relations are a key item on New Zealand's political
agenda, because they are defined as a problem. The argument is that the media
contribute significantly to this.

New Zealand's evolving race relations

After the outright conflict of the Anglo-Maori wars of last century, the relationship between Maori and Pakeha was relatively subdued and contact was limited.
The Maori population declined, owing to the effects of disease, substandard living
conditions and conflict. Sheer survival became a priority for Maori, leaders and
people alike. Maori tended to be primarily located in the provincial towns and
rural areas. Pakeha, by contrast, were increasingly located in the major urban
areas where they forged ahead with the new order of capitalism. From the turn
of the century until the Second World War, Maori and Pakeha tended to live
separate lives within New Zealand. Social intercourse was most likely to occur
when the Maori were required for domestic labour in the home or as workers
in the freezing industry, as shearers or agricultural harvesters, or in other
menial jobs.

The Second World War changed this situation irrevocably. Maori and Pakeha
were thrown into much closer contact by the requirements of the war effort. Maori
became essential to the New Zealand contribution both at home and abroad. At
the end of the war, influenced by their experiences during the war, many Maori
chose to migrate to the urban areas. From 1945, this migration was encouraged
by the Government, who saw no future for the Maori in the rural areas but

recognised they were vital to the establishment and growth of urban-based industries that marked the post-war period.

The 1950s and 1960s saw the establishment of the key ingredients in contemporary race relations: migrant Maori (and later Pacific Island) communities in particular localities of the major urban centres, supplying unskilled and semi-skilled labour for an industrial economy. But there was little to indicate what this might mean for the future. The economic optimism of the 1950s and 1960s produced a corresponding optimism about race relations. The conformity and stability of those decades was not disturbed by the new contact between Maori and Pakeha. The racism which did occur was unlikely to attract the media's attention.

The challenge, when it came, developed rapidly. By the late 1960s, there were new generations of Maori who had spent a major part, if not all, of their lives in Auckland or Wellington, and a few were beginning to percolate through to tertiary education institutions. They were part of the post-war baby boom that was to have such an impact as consumers and as a political force. They introduced new political ideas and strategies. The effect was apparent in the activism of the late 1960s which used mass public demonstrations to oppose New Zealand's involvement in the Vietnam war. The liberal values of popular music, along with the new wave of feminism and the civil rights movement in the United States, also had an influence on these evolving politics.

Maori political organisations were rapidly established as separate entities. In 1969 and 1970, important new groups appeared. Particularly notable was Nga Tamatoa, which began at the University of Auckland in 1970. Such groups were influential in importing arguments about institutional racism from the United States, in developing a political philosophy which was highly critical of the dominant Pakeha for their treatment of Maori values and institutions, and in demanding that consideration be given to unresolved issues such as Maori land and the Treaty of Waitangi. Maori provided leadership in the debates and activities that were to follow (see Ranginui Walker's chapter for further material).

The 1970s were marked by a series of highly visible protests on the questions of Maori land and language. There were annual demonstrations at Waitangi Day ceremonies, and a well-publicised land march in 1975. Land in rural communities was the subject of disputes about ownership and access, but so too was land in the major urban centres. The occupation of Bastion Point in Auckland in 1977 and 1978 reinforced the concerns of Maori at the continued loss of their land. At the end of the 1970s, few New Zealanders could reasonably claim ignorance of the take (agenda) of the now organised and articulate Maori political groups that existed.

The 1980s have seen these concerns increasingly reflected in public policy, most notably in public sector management and service delivery. In 1982-83, the arguments of Maori sovereignty were published in the feminist magazine *Broadsheet*. Although they were not the only statements to be made on the clash between Maori and European cultural and economic systems, or the need to re-establish Maori independence in New Zealand, the Maori sovereignty articles (published later as a book) became something of a manifesto for political change. The audience were liberal and radical Pakeha in various social service occupations — teaching, social work, nursing, probation, and so on.

In the wake of the 1981 Springbok rugby tour of New Zealand, activism was channeled towards an examination of local institutions and systems, and the ways in which Maori were disadvantaged. This focus is evidenced in such reports as the 1985 WARAG review of institutional racism in the Department of Social Welfare in Auckland, and then by the far-reaching *Puao-Te-Atatu*, the Ministerial Advisory Committee's report on a Maori perspective for the Department of Social Welfare. The previously defined 'radical' calls to address matters of institutional racism, the Treaty of Waitangi and biculturalism were receiving attention in central reviews of major government departments supported by senior management and prominent Maori. Even documents such as Treasury's 1987 *Government Management: A Brief to the Incoming Government* give the Treaty of Waitangi prominence, although this recognition is somewhat marred by Treasury's attempt to reinterpret the Treaty in a way favourable to its own ideological view.

This new climate was reflected in major policy changes initiated by Government and some state departments. Reform had begun in 1977, when the Department of Maori Affairs had initiated what appeared to be a devolution in certain management and policy-making processes. Maori communities were given a new authority to guide what was done in their locality. Additionally, innovative and positive developments occurred in Maori language retention (kohanga reo), youth care (maatua whangai) and skills training (kokiri). Perhaps the next most significant initiative was the amendment which allowed the Waitangi Tribunal to investigate complaints back to 1840. The Tribunal was still only able to recommend action to the Government, but now it provided a forum for longstanding complaints about unfair land dealings. It also began to adopt a more assertive stance, beginning with the Motonui finding, which directly questioned the Government's actions. The Tribunal was providing a challenge to both the notion of 'one law for all' and the Labour Government's economic policies.[2] The Tribunal has helped lay a foundation for legal and political pluralism[3] and in the process has provoked something of a crisis in the corporatisation of government departments and the move to privatise the fishing resources of New Zealand. For these and other reasons, the Tribunal has been the target for the unease of many Pakeha and has been held responsible for the intensified conflict over ethnic identity.

During the 1970s, as attention was focused on Maori concerns, Pacific Island migrant communities were also coming in for their share of attention. The New Zealand economy began a decline from 1973, and Pacific Islanders became a scapegoat as Pakeha sought to identify the cause. The negative label of 'overstayer' became synonymous with Pacific Islander, especially Samoans and Tongans, and unemployment, a deterioration in law and order and the problem areas of the major cities were all associated with the presence of Pacific Islanders. If Maori had to fight for their rights as an indigenous people, Pacific Islanders had to fight for their very right to be here. Their political activities therefore centred on immigration laws and policies.

Current debates and issues

The developments of the 1970s and 1980s have placed race relations in the centre of public debate in New Zealand. The question of national and ethnic identity and the implications for the distribution of resources are highly contentious issues. In terms of a national identity, New Zealand is in a transition stage, with competing loyalties and a great deal of confusion. At the same time as groups such as Nga Tamatoa were being established, Britain was turning its attention away from the Empire and opting to enter the European Community. For pragmatic economic reasons, New Zealand had to seek new alliances and markets. Traditional enemies became major trading partners. Asia and the Pacific, from necessity rather than choice, became more important. But the contradictions of an Anglophile nation deep in the South Pacific are far from being resolved. New Zealand does not see itself committed to Asia in the way that Australia does, and relations with the micro-states of the South Pacific are still less important in both a political and economic sense than relations with a number of northern hemisphere countries.

There is still indecision and some confusion over this sense of identity, and there is a marked contrast between Maori and Pakeha over how they conceive of themselves in a cultural sense. Maori have politicised ethnicity, or cultural identity, in the last decades, and on the basis of a new confidence in their own identity, have made claims for equal consideration in the allocation of resources. The touchstone has been the Treaty of Waitangi. In a society that values legal agreements and the order imposed by legal structures, the Treaty is an important weapon in arguing for equity for Maori. The Treaty, and its dismissal for more than a hundred years, is used to remind the dominant Pakeha group of its obligations.

In a parallel development, the notion of biculturalism (and bilingualism) challenges Pakeha to explore the possibility of establishing a degree of partnership between Maori and Pakeha. The critique of existing arrangements, which accompanies notions such as institutional racism, helps reinforce the demands for biculturalism and the need to acknowledge the Treaty of Waitangi. But the criticism of dominant institutions, of the continuing links to Britain and the need to restructure New Zealand society, or at least major parts of it, has intensified the confusion of Pakeha in a period of major social and economic change. For many (probably most) Pakeha, the debate over cultural identity and equity for Maori is deeply threatening.

Pakeha do not have a conception of themselves as a distinct cultural or ethnic group — that is, distinct from Maori or various Pacific Island groups, but also from the Europeans who settled in Australia or Canada. As a rule, Pakeha have considerable difficulty in identifying what features (language, behaviour, values, rituals) make them culturally distinctive. Even 'Pakeha' is a highly contested label, and the preferred alternatives, 'European' or 'New Zealander', highlight the confusion. The assertiveness of Maori cultural politics has underlined these problems. Biculturalism may be the preferred option for Maori, but the term assumes that Pakeha have a sense of who they are and what they can contribute as a partner. So Pakeha unease, fed by institutions such as the media, has led to a negative and often reactionary response.

Any developments that give Maoritanga a greater role in this society have received a far from enthusiastic response from Pakeha. Taha Maori in the education system has been opposed by Christian conservatives for its spiritual content which is perceived as a threat to Christianity. Others simply view Maori content of whatever sort in education as irrelevant to the needs of a modern industrial society, as a cover for liberal/radical ideas, and as unable to guarantee jobs. Similar arguments are used in the case against Maori as an official language. In the area of criminal activity and public order, 'gangs', which are incorrectly identified as almost solely Maori, have been seen as epitomising the general decline in discipline and morality. And to exacerbate these concerns, the possibility of economic resources going to Maori, notably with regard to fisheries and land, has greatly angered many Pakeha.

The evidence of this growing Pakeha hostility is not difficult to find. Public opinion polls show some support for a greater emphasis on the Treaty of Waitangi, especially before the debates about land and fisheries resources which occurred in 1988, but opposition when it comes to translating this support into practical options. Groups such as the Concerned Parents Association and the Coalition of Concerned Citizens have been active nationally and in a number of specific communities in opposing taha Maori in schools. Here there is a definition of taha Maori as anti-Christian. Different reasons but the same opposition can be found in publications such as *Metro*. (In fairness to *Metro*, it consistently publishes opposing viewpoints on race relations.)

In the case of economic resources, self-interested groups appealed to public opinion to gain a mandate to stop Maori access to such resources. In mid-1988, Bob Martin, a fishing industry leader, began a public campaign to undermine Maori claims and Waitangi Tribunal recommendations concerning fisheries. Later he was joined by the One New Zealand Foundation, which has aggressively sought to deny minority ethnicity and to promote the myth of a 'one New Zealand' identity.

Given the confusion of many Pakeha over such issues, this narrow notion of nationalism is very popular. The oft-stated phrase 'We are all New Zealanders' is used as a counter to those who would argue that 'being Maori' or 'being Samoan' is important. The statement implies a unity where none exists, now or in the past, and provides a relatively underhand means of expressing old forms of prejudice. The standard arguments about there being no full-blooded Maori left (as though it were relevant) have been combined with new arguments about a New Zealand-style apartheid which privileges Maori and disadvantages Pakeha. Calls are increasing for the abolition of the Waitangi Tribunal, the Office of the Race Relations Conciliator, and any other body which exists to protect Maori interests. In addition, there is a denial that the Treaty of Waitangi has any contemporary relevance. Many Pakeha, led by groups such as the One New Zealand Foundation, have gone on the offensive.

Racism and the media

The present tension creates substantial difficulties for the media. It is an emotionally charged situation in which the major participants seldom have intimate contact with one another. But the media must also take some responsibility for the state of contemporary race relations. Their failure to convey accurately and fairly the circumstances and issues of race relations has exacerbated communal tension, especially where there is little first-hand experience with which to contradict media reporting. The media's power to 'create' facts and confirm values makes them a significant, if not *the* significant, factor in influencing public opinion. The print, audio and audio-visual media determine how we understand other groups in our society, and will reinforce or contradict the views held by one person or another.

If the media get things wrong, they create an impression which is very difficult to counter. But there are also certain limitations to the media's influence. People are not passive, and while the media reinforce prejudice, they seldom create it (see previous chapter). And if the media are racist, then it will be because the wider society is racist. The media will reflect and appeal to commonly held values to varying degrees. If racism is part of New Zealand society, then it would be unusual not to find it represented in the media.

New Zealand lacks detailed research on the role of the media in causing or contributing to racism, but research from other countries tends to show a definite link. One of the most authoritative (though now dated) research projects was carried out in Britain by Hartmann and Husband.

> They argue that the important effect of the mass media is not that watching television makes us more violent or permissive or racist, but that the media throw some features into sharp relief, obliterate others, select and limit the issues which are worthy of consideration or recall. The mass media do not determine attitudes, but they do structure and select information we may use on which to base decisions about what attitude is appropriate.[4]

The researchers found that the media in Britain perpetuated negative perceptions of Afro-Caribbeans and Asians, and the overwhelming image was that race relations involved intergroup *conflict*. This image and information served to legitimate the existing views of readers, listeners or viewers, and the process became circular — public opinion held negative views of non-whites and saw them as a problem; this was reflected in media coverage and comment, thereby reinforcing the originally held views. Hartmann and Husband also discovered that negative views were most likely to come from those who had no direct personal contact with either Afro-Caribbeans or Asians and who had to rely for their information on the media. Those who were more likely to see conflict as epitomising race relations usually cited the media as the source of their information.

Ironically, recent American research[5] shows that television plays an important role in convincing minority groups (in this case, Afro-Americans) that there is more racial integration than their direct experience would suggest. Highly segregated residential patterns and the message of black political movements reinforce the Afro-American belief that racial integration is a myth. But those blacks who watch a lot of television, irrespective of their education, age, residential location or community involvement, believe that there is a significant level of racial integration in United States society because of the images presented on television. Programmes such as *The Cosby Show* 'epitomise the Afro-American dream of full acceptance and assimilation in US society'.[6] As Maharey argues (see previous chapter), the audience reacts to the media in different ways. While significant numbers in the majority group may have their negative views of others reinforced, minority groups might well take a very different message from the media. If the American research is an indicator, minority groups may be persuaded that the situation is better than their own experience suggests. The mitigating factor in New Zealand is that there are no local equivalents to *The Cosby Show* or *Frank's Place*.

The media determine what becomes public knowledge, thereby influencing opinions and values. The media reinforce negative views about minority groups, and intergroup relations generally, by the way in which they present information. Their need to report what has happened in a truncated form inevitably means that decisions are made about what is worth reporting. It is this tendency to present, at best, a partial picture, and at worst, a distorted one, and to do so to outsiders who are not in a position to judge the accuracy of the reporting, that invites widespread criticism of the media's handling of race relations. It is compounded by the coincidence of the media's information with prejudice and racism in the community, and by the inability of minority groups to counter the images and 'facts' offered via the media. Many groups (of all sorts of political persuasions and ethnic origin) feel that their activities and feelings are constantly misreported and that they have no adequate right of reply.

People who live in largely segregated communities (these may be social rather than strictly geographical), and who lack the knowledge that comes from direct contact, tend to rely exclusively on the media. The media reinforce incorrect images of other groups. For instance, the activities of politicians, the police, the Department of Immigration and the media unfairly created an image of Pacific Islanders as overstayers. This association was first established in the mid-1970s when overstayers were cast as a substantial social problem for New Zealand. But the image has continued as public folklore justifying the discriminatory activities of the Immigration Department.[7]

The inaccuracy can be simply demonstrated. In 1985 and 1986, Pacific Island overstayers constituted less than one-third of all overstayers, while overstayers from the United States and the United Kingdom constituted another third. These figures are contrary to commonly held beliefs. But the matter was compounded by the fact that in the same period 86 percent of all prosecutions against overstayers involved Pacific Islanders, while only 5 percent involved American or British overstayers.[8] The media, in repeating rather than challenging a highly inaccurate public image (with some exceptions, see chapter 15), have seriously contributed to inter-group hostility and helped produce a blanket anti-Pacific Islander feeling amongst many Pakeha.

This negative media role has been demonstrated in their treatment of a range of other events and groups, as later chapters in this book will illustrate. The shorthand style of the media's reporting of events is a fundamental problem. It starts with the one-word definitions used by the media to categorise people. A label such as activist/radical/protester/demonstrator automatically invokes a negative perception. Those, such as Atareta Poananga or Titewhai Harawira, who are labelled in this way become folk devils to the extent that they are used to illustrate the 'excesses' of Maori activism. Their comments and activities become a caricature, and even in reports where the labels are not used, the convention is sufficiently well established for the reader, viewer or listener to supply the appropriate label for themselves.

Headlines are a useful guide both to the shorthand used by, in this case, the print media and to their values. Headlines, because of their brevity and their role in encouraging sales of a journal or paper or in attracting a reader to a particular item, need to use unambiguous and attention-seeking terms. The headlines also set up the reader's approach to a particular story, and some newspapers make a practice of using headlines that make claims which are not justified by the text of the report. Headlines provide a concise and value-laden indication of a publication's stance on a particular issue. In recent years, New Zealand race relations have been characterised, in headline format, as conflict-ridden, with so-called 'Maori issues' cast as the threat. The following illustrate the point:

'TREATY BILL COULD FORCE OUT FARMER'
New Zealand Herald, 27/1/88
'TRIBUNAL TO HEAR CLAIM FOR BIG SLICE OF THE WAIKATO'
New Zealand Herald, 20/1/88
'MAORI CLAIMS THREAT TO ELECTRICITY'
New Zealand Herald, 3/2/88
'FISHERIES FACE MAORI RIGHTS THREAT'
Auckland Star, 28/7/88

In these instances, the media establish very clear images through the association of ethnic issues and conflict words such as 'threat'. This style becomes even more obvious when the reporting of violent offending is considered. A modest survey of the media[9] produced two very apparent conclusions. First, words which describe the ethnicity of the dominant group (Pakeha, European) are infrequently used when compared with the use of labels such as Maori, Pacific Islander or Polynesian. The latter are used three to four times more than the former in newspapers. Secondly, this has been particularly true of violent and sexual offending. Even when allowance is made for the disproportionate number of Maori and Pacific Islanders involved in such offences, the newspapers still exaggerate their involvement by the frequent use of ethnic labels *when the perpetrator is Polynesian*.

Some of the blame for this sort of publicity can be attributed to politicians, especially those who seek to dramatise race relations by appealing to public prejudices. For example, the questioning of the Waitangi Tribunal's impartiality by the Leader of the Opposition (*New Zealand Herald*, 2/2/88), Rob Muldoon's comment on 'race relations fear' (*Sunday Star*, 20/3/88) or Trevor de Cleene's claim[10] that 'activists speed Pakeha exodus to Queensland' (*Herald*, 21/7/88) — note that activism is automatically associated with Maori, fear with Pakeha — do not add much that is positive to the public debate. Such comments at times invite unfair criticism of the media who have simply been the vehicle for such political claims. But equally, the media themselves contribute significantly to these political messages. The 'kill a white' incident at the University of Auckland marae was initially reported in a dubious manner, but the media subsequently contributed little by way of corrective accurate information.[11]

Two other examples of the media's putting a particular interpretation on events will suffice. The *Northland Times* (15/4/88) ran a headline, 'World Judaism Shamed/Bestial Israelis Switch to Death Camp Tactics'. The Press Council ruled that the text of the article did not refer to the reaction of world Judaism or justify the reference to death camp tactics. (The Press Council declined to rule that the headline might have been offensive to Jews, however, a stance which is difficult to understand.) The second example is from a report in the *New Zealand Herald* (6/1/88) on how the Member for the Bay of Islands was settling into Parliament. The headline was 'Race Tension in North Close to Flashpoint', with claims made about the racial conflict said to exist in his electorate. Here, a politician's comments are given a very particular, and negative, emphasis. It is the selection and presentation of these comments, a media responsibility, that has cast race relations as disorder news. So much of the abnormal referred to tends to have the label 'Maori' attached.

This preoccupation with conflict and disaster in many areas, not only in the area of race relations, highlights the news values of the media. It is reflected in the media-speak of the headlines and the media's in-house guidelines for deciding what should be included and how it ought to be portrayed. In this way, the media directly contribute to public perceptions of what constitutes our society, and how we ought to understand events and groups. If race relations are widely defined as involving conflict and tension, then the media will have played a central role in creating and sustaining that dominant image.

The following comments exemplify both the news values of people in the media and their resistance to those who would criticise their coverage of race relations. The first statement is from the editor of the daily news for TVNZ; the second from the network news editor.

Brown:
A news story today where there is conflict is Maori fishing. All right, Sweet [previously critical of the news as being a reflection of the white male system] might say we should not do this story because it is conflict. I take the opposing view: it's a story we must do because it's conflict and a conflict that needs to be resolved, and you'll only resolve the conflict by informing people about it. There is nothing wrong with a healthy tension in society that we reflect.

Cutler:
We are not in the business of reporting the norm, we are in the business of reporting the abnormal.[12]

These comments underline the argument that the coverage of race relations is structured by certain media values. For instance, many in the media assume that race relations, by their nature, involve conflict. The resulting negative and often inaccurate coverage filters the information available to the public, and if the overseas research is valid for New Zealand, then public racism is directly reinforced by the activities of the media. The guiding values and assumptions of the media reflect a variety of factors: the need to accommodate, at least to some degree, the views of the targeted buyer or advertisers; the news and entertainment values that predominate amongst those who control or work in the media; the nature of the media, which produces superficial coverage on many occasions; and the lack of appropriate skills amongst those who work in the media — especially little or no understanding of te reo Maori or taha Maori.[13]

With the changing nature of race relations in New Zealand in the 1970s and 1980s, the media have been challenged on some of these matters and have responded. There have on occasions been skilled journalists who have had an impact in developing a better public understanding of key race relations issues. But in general the intensified nature of the intergroup conflict, especially over issues such as biculturalism and resources such as land or fisheries, has been fed by media coverage. The media are a major influence on how people understand race relations, and if matters have got worse, then the media must assume responsibility. They are not the only factor but they are certainly one of the most important.

Access to the media

One matter that exacerbates the situation is the lack of options available to those who do not have access to the media. When reporting is inaccurate, there are few avenues of redress (letters to the editor, press release, complaint to the Press Council, legal action) and most take time, are still at the discretion of those who are the subject of the complaint and if a correction does eventuate, it seldom receives the same prominence as the earlier offending item. It is not only that many ethnic groups feel their position has been misreported; they are often excluded from the news altogether, especially when what they have to say, or what has happened, shows them in a positive light. The media reserve for themselves the right to judge what is newsworthy and what is entertaining.

One option, if there is dissatisfaction with the media, is to create separate institutions whereby more appropriate coverage of Maori events and issues, for example, can be provided. This allows the mass media to be sidestepped. Publications such as Black Power's *Te Iwi o Aotearoa* or the radio station Te Upoko o te Ika are moves to provide alternative channels of communication. Information is not filtered and reinterpreted. The link between the Maori community and the medium is direct and unhindered. But the option of separate media faces substantial political opposition from Pakeha, the public, politicians and broadcasting alike.[14] As long as there is Pakeha involvement, there will be compromises which will undercut the effectiveness of Maori radio, television or publishing.

In the United States, the civil rights movement produced a greater awareness of the media's racism, of the underemployment of blacks in the industry and of their lack of access to policy decisionmaking. This awareness was heightened by racial conflict during the 1960s and the findings of groups such as the Kerner Commission that the media had contributed to the escalation of tension and violence. (Similar developments occurred in Britain.[15]) The Federal Community Commission, which is an independent government agency whose job is to regulate the US telecommunications industry, has responded by promoting change in order to help blacks. But the effect has been to employ blacks in highly visible positions without any decisionmaking power, and the appearance of new black shows (for example, *The Cosby Show*) that are colour-blind address few issues of importance to blacks. Meanwhile the media continue to be dominated by the interests of whites and the business community in recognition of those who are the prime investors in the high-price telecommunications market. Black concerns continue to be ignored and blacks lack the investment capital to effectively create their own networks.[16]

There are other options where alternative media cannot be contemplated because of a lack of finance capital. Those who are currently employed in the media could be encouraged to re-evaluate their competence. In the United Kingdom, for example, journalists have played an important role in monitoring the media's racism. The National Union of Journalists set up a race relations working party in 1974. The Campaign Against Racism in the Media (which began work in 1976) and the Black Media Workers' Association (1981), along with the NUJ working party, have encouraged sensitivity among those who work in the media. The National Union of Journalists has clear guidelines about reporting race relations in its Code of Conduct, and provides the working party with a budget to see that issues of racism are addressed. It is an important step, especially as journalists are reluctant to admit to error.[17] Racism is as much an emotive and threatening issue for journalists as it is for the public in general.

Conclusion

Race relations in New Zealand have changed significantly since the 1950s and 1960s. The issues have become much more politically charged as notions of identity and the distribution of resources based on these identities are renegotiated. At a time when we have a much better analysis of racism in New Zealand society, and groups are working to confront racism, the level of public and political racism is increasing. That is to say, it has moved from the relatively private confines of the home or private gathering to the public arenas of politics, commerce and social service delivery. Many Pakeha feel uncomfortable with the charges of racism but feel equally that Maori demands are unreasonable and that 'Maori privilege' is a predominant form of racism in New Zealand. In this charged and emotive environment, the media play an important role as the most significant channels of information. They can continue to reinforce the prejudice of Pakeha, or they can help challenge ideas and opinions.

The activities of the media are critical to the success or failure of an equitable and democratic society. This is particularly true in the area of race relations.

> The coverage of race relations and immigration presents newspapers with an enormous professional challenge: how to ensure that genuinely differing viewpoints can be expressed and reflected in such an emotive field without helping to incite . . . conflict. . . . A healthy democracy depends upon the availability of facts and the clash of opinion about them.[18]

It has been argued here that many of the 'facts' made available via the media are incomplete, inaccurate or misleading, and that the full range of opinion, especially that from Maori and minority ethnic groups, is not represented in the media. When the integrity of the material available in the media is challenged in this way, it has critical implications for social progress, equity and the nature of democracy. If the media distort public utterances and debate, then the freedom of the *press* becomes an enemy of the freedom of *speech*.[19]

Chapter 3

THE ROLE OF THE PRESS IN DEFINING PAKEHA PERCEPTIONS OF THE MAORI

Ranginui Walker

The growth of an unequal relationship

The relationship that exists between the Maori as the tangata whenua of New Zealand and the Pakeha who settled in the country in the last 150 years is one of social, political and economic subjection. This unequal relationship is derived from the process of colonisation by an industrialised imperial nation of a tribal people isolated for a thousand years. Under the Treaty of Waitangi, well-armed and numerically superior tribes agreed to the British Crown's establishing kawanatanga, or government, to secure order between the tribes, and to control the 2000 or so British nationals resident in the country.

The coloniser interpreted the concession to govern as a cession of sovereignty which warded off other potential metropolitan claimants, such as France. But the Treaty conferred only notional sovereignty, which the Governor over time translated into real sovereignty. For their part, the chiefs believed their own sovereignty, or mana, was protected by the Crown's guarantee, in Article 2 of the Treaty, of chieftainship over their lands, forests, fisheries and treasured possessions. They were soon to be disillusioned.

The critical steps in the subjection of the Maori and the expropriation of their resources were taken by Governor Grey. First he introduced an aggressive land-buying policy to extinguish native title by 'fair purchase'. His purchase of the whole of the South Island, by 1858, and substantive areas in the North Island, allowed settlers to flood in, outnumber the Maori, and dominate them politically when representative government was established in 1854. The exclusion of Maori from the General Assembly by a franchise based on individual property, when most Maori land was in tribal ownership, allowed Parliament to pass laws to the detriment of the Maori without a dissenting voice being raised. These measures included making war on Wiremu Kingi in Taranaki to settle a civil dispute, extending the war to Waikato, and passing the New Zealand Settlements Act (1863) to confiscate 3 million acres of Maori land for Pakeha settlers. But Maori were formidable military opponents who inflicted many defeats on the British Army, and war as a means of acquiring land was abandoned. After the major campaign in Waikato and the Bay of Plenty ended in 1864, more subtle techniques were adopted to alienate the remaining 16 million acres of land still held by the Maori in the North Island.

The first measure in this new strategy was the Maori Representation Act (1867), which established four Maori seats in Parliament. On a population basis, the Maori were entitled to 20 seats in a House of 70 members. But such a sizable block of votes would have been inimical to Pakeha designs on Maori land. The second measure was the Native Land Act (1867), which established the Native Land Court. The Court functioned to break up tribal land holdings into individual ownership, thereby facilitating purchase from the 10 or so 'owners' named on the certificate of title. The rest of the tribe were dispossessed. By 1900, only 5 million acres of land (of the 66 million they once owned) remained in Maori ownership, and these remnants were further reduced by subsequent legislation, which culminated in the 1967 Maori Affairs Amendment Act. This measure, dubbed the 'last land grab' by Maori leaders, provided for the compulsory purchase of 'uneconomic' Maori land and transferred Maori land owned by fewer than three people into European hands. By this time, most Maori had been reduced to penury and forced to migrate to towns and cities in search of work. Only 3 million acres of land remained in Maori ownership.

The Maori stoutly resisted colonial despoliation — by defending their land against invasion, by guerrilla warfare, by petitions to the British Sovereign, and by political means such as the formation of Maori parliaments. But these efforts are not part of the collective memory of the Pakeha New Zealander. Attempts at accommodation with the colonising power by educated Maori leaders such as Buck, Ngata, and Pomare after the turn of the century were interpreted by the Pakeha as signalling Maori acceptance of their subordinate place in society.

Maori served the Crown in two world wars, but in general remained isolated from Pakeha in rural tribal hinterlands. Nonetheless the Pakeha fostered and promulgated to the world a myth of racial harmony in New Zealand that was not shattered until the 1970s. By that time, 70 percent of the Maori population had left their rural homes. In the span of one generation, the centre of gravity of Maori society had shifted to the towns and cities. In the urban milieu, Maori culture flourished, with the development of cultural clubs and sports teams and the building of urban marae. The transition from rural to urban life also resulted in Maori people adopting political action in response to Pakeha control over their lives.

Politicisation by city-educated radicals had its impact on Maori society. But the rising tide of Maori activism was identified through the news media with a few disaffected young radicals disturbing social harmony and dividing the races. On the issue of race relations, the Fourth Estate represented establishment thinking and functioned to maintain the status quo — that is, Maori subordination.

The 'haka party' incident

Contemporary Maori activism began with the emergence in 1970 of Nga Tamatoa — the Young Warriors. Their annual protest at the Treaty of Waitangi celebrations triggered the Maori Land March of 1975 and the occupation of Bastion Point in 1977. Both the Land March and the Bastion Point protests were characterised by passive resistance and, accordingly, treated in a generally benign way by the news media. But an incident in 1979 brought a very different response.

At the University of Auckland a small group of activists took violent direct action to put a stop to the racist parody of the haka performed there annually by engineering students. For years Maori had attempted to negotiate an end to the event. Nonetheless, by failing to remain passive, in their assigned subordinate position, they presented a threat the state could not tolerate, as was implicit in the media treatment of the incident.

In May 1979, the *Auckland Star* reported the haka party incident with the bold headline 'Gang rampage at varsity, Students at haka practice bashed'. The headline was sensationalist and inaccurate. There wasn't a single gang patch in evidence during the incident, yet no headline could have evoked a more emotive response from the general public. The patch-wearing gang member is the incarnation of the worst fears of the Pakeha.

The first Polynesian gang to appear on the Auckland scene, in 1970, were the Stormtroopers, whose denim uniforms and swastika emblems symbolised their alienation from mainstream society. Thereafter other gangs, such as Black Power, the Mongrel Mob and the Headhunters, came to public notice as they engaged in fraternal battles over territory. Fighting each other was one thing, but a 'gang' invading the hallowed precincts of a university was viewed as intolerable.

The public, according to the media, demanded retribution. Editors pontificated — 'No Place for Violence' (*New Zealand Herald*, 3/5/79), 'A Racial Farce' (*Dominion*, 4/5/79). Maori leaders such as Harry Dansey, the Race Relations Conciliator, and Dr Peter Sharples, his executive officer, came under immediate pressure from newspapers to disavow violence and thereby isolate the offenders. The headline over their comments on the issue read 'Attack on Students Condemned' (*Herald*, 2/5/79). Sharples' rider to his disapproval of violence — that most of Maoridom would support the stand against the haka — was played down.

Not until the *Star* (28/5/79) reported the Auckland District Maori Council's reasons for providing 'Maori Help for the Haka Attack Group' was it made clear that there was other than a Pakeha view of the incident. Even so, when the haka party case went to court, it was reported by both the *Herald* (6/7/79) and the *Star* (6/7/79) as a 'light-hearted' stunt. Only two writers put the issue in its context of racism. These were W. P. Reeves, in his piece 'Rough Ride to Racism' (*Dominion*, 18/5/79), and Tony Reid, in an editorial headed 'Mocking the Maori' (*Listener*, 26/5/79).

After the court hearing against the He Taua defendants, respected Maori leaders argued that cultural violence by Pakeha students precipitated physical violence in retaliation. Finally the press began to understand the issue. When the Human Rights Commission produced its report on the incident, more discerning headlines began to appear — 'Cherished Myth of Racial Harmony', 'After the Haka . . . Whither New Zealand?' (*Herald*, 10/4/80), 'The Haka Party Incident and Beyond' (*Star*, 10/4/80).

Maranga Mai

Although Pakeha perceptions of the haka party affair may have evolved, complacency towards the Maori remained. A year later, when young activists dramatised Maori land grievances in the play *Maranga Mai*, performed at Mangere

College in Auckland, again the negative response of some Pakeha was given prominent treatment. The *Herald* headline read 'School Angry after Show by Maori Group' (3/5/80). The *Star* wrote 'Angry Minister Calls for Ban on Play Group' (5/5/80). The play reputedly disturbed 'race feelings'. Merv Wellington, the Minister of Education, pressured the Manukau City Council to ban *Maranga Mai* performances from schools in its area.

The opinion of a Pakeha city councillor, Peter Aldridge, on Maori reaction was given prominent treatment under the headline 'Maori Parents Intimidated on Play' (*Star*, 7/5/80). Mr Aldridge's right to speak on behalf of Maori was not challenged by the press, though mention was made of the president of the Labour Party, Jim Anderton's comments that the violent reaction to the play should be 'treated with the contempt it deserved' (*Star*, 7/5/80).

The press's negative treatment of Maori actions aimed at redressing their grievances precipitated a witchhunt. The *Herald* ran the headline 'Manukau Council Wants Report on Show' (6/5/80). The actions of the city council's detached youth worker, Brian Lepou, in arranging the play's performance were closely scrutinised by the city manager. The Department of Internal Affairs, which paid Lepou's salary, was also asked to investigate the matter. The overreaction by Pakeha authorities and slanted sensationalist treatment by the press could only be interpreted by Maori as Pakeha intolerance of attempts to confront them with the past. Perhaps they understood the power of drama to change people's political perceptions. In any case, the power-brokers and the media made common cause in loud public condemnation of *Maranga Mai*. By the time of the play's finale, at a special performance in the Beehive theatrette four months later, the *Herald* was trumpeting 'Urban Guerrilla Play Stuns Beehive' (2/9/80).

Underlying Pakeha opposition to *Maranga Mai* was the fear that Maori activism and politicisation would generate revolt. The end result of this control over Maori by both Pakeha power structures and the media is a distorted perception of reality in society. Maori efforts to politicise the Pakeha, as well as their own people, about injustice are denigrated. Calls for recognition of the principles of the Treaty of Waitangi are submerged in Pakeha self-interest.

Waitangi action

For 10 years, Maori protest activity at the annual Treaty of Waitangi celebrations provided the press with good copy and ample ammunition to portray the protesters in a negative light. In 1981, when the investiture of Dame Whina Cooper and Sir Graham Latimer was held on Waitangi Marae, the press had a field-day. Protesters objected to the investiture taking place on the marae, and the presence of the Pakeha Governor-General whose predecessors had dishonoured the Treaty. The noisy but peaceful protest was reported under the headline 'Waitangi Marae in Uproar as Police Arrest Eight' (*Herald*, 7/2/81). The *Star*'s headline declared 'Police, Activists Brawl on Marae' (6/2/81). Protesters were arrested for crying 'shame' during the investiture. Police intervened in what they declared to be 'an emergency situation' — 'People's lives were at stake. It could have erupted in a full-scale riot.' Media coverage of the protest reinforced a public perception of the protest as a violent affair. The depiction of the protesters as villains in the socio-drama between Maori and Pakeha on that Waitangi Day was supported by the reporting of Prime Minister Muldoon's view that the protesters were 'outcasts' in Maori society (*Herald*, 7/2/81).

Ten months after the event, riot charges against the seven protesters charged over the Waitangi protest were dismissed in the Kaikohe District Court. Judge Paul's finding that, contrary to reported accounts, not one stone had been thrown or stick wielded in a manner that would constitute a riot, did little to influence the original public perception of the protest. For those who were present, and who read the judgement, it was apparent that the media reports had distorted the event.

The media and the gangs

While the activists were the cutting edge of Maori society seeking social change, gangs as organisations for the dispossessed alienated brown proletariat were the achilles heel, always vulnerable to Pakeha counter-attack. In the seventies, the police operated as neutral observers of territorial gang fights, intervening only when necessary to investigate a homicide or robbery committed by gang members. But in 1979, the police were drawn into a confrontation with the Stormtroopers in the car park of the Moerewa Hotel. The incident culminated in a violent assault on the police, the burning of a police van, and the shooting of a gang member. Headlines such as 'Kill, Kill, Kill!', 'Northland Nurses Its Wounds after a Weekend of Violence' (*Herald*, 6/8/79) and 'Shotguns Trained on Gangs' (*Star*, 6/8/79) roused deep public fears and hostility towards gangs. Even the president of the Maori Council felt impelled to call for a 'crackdown' on gang violence (*Herald*, 28/10/80).

When the government committee on gangs, chaired by Under-Secretary for Internal Affairs Ken Comber, reported in May 1981, the heat surrounding the affair had been somewhat dissipated by community meetings in Northland. Revelations of high unemployment and analyses by researchers and detached youth workers assigned to gangs gave a context to the violence, which was seen as symptomatic of complex underlying social problems arising out of family break-down, alienation, school failure and chronic unemployment. The Comber committee report warned that the news media were responsible for promulgating more negative images of gangs than was justified. It said a cursory study of media reporting suggested that coverage was intense but poorly balanced on gang-related issues (*Herald*, 13/5/81). The enduring public perception of gangs remains one of bestial behaviour and gratuitous violence, a situation often not helped by the gangs themselves. The Mongrel Mob reinforced that perception when a young woman was snatched off the street and raped in Mangere at the gang's Ambury Park convention in 1986.

The gang rape became a media cause célèbre. Outraged citizens of Mangere threatened dire consequences to members of the Auckland Regional Authority for permitting the use of the Ambury Park site for a gang convention. The community was reported to be 'Out for ARA Blood' (*Herald*, 15/12/86). MPs urged government action to give police stronger powers to deal with gangs (*Herald*, 16/12/86). But the political ripples at the local level were much more compelling.

Gang leaders felt obliged to take their own punitive action against the gang, irrespective of what the law did in bringing the guilty individuals to justice, since the whole gang, comprising chapters from all over the country, bore the stigma of the event.

The ARA parks committee chairman threatened retaliation against the Auckland chapter of the Mongrel Mob by withdrawing from its Nga Kuri Rohe Potae work trust a three-month, $30,000 contract (*Star*, 16/12/86). This chapter of the Mob, under the leadership of Tuhoe Isaacs, had called for a moratorium on criminal activities so as to establish a work trust for its members and emulate the achievement of the successful Black Power gang with its work trust, 'factory' and night club headquarters in East Tamaki. The report 'Gang Finds Pride through Work', in which Black Power leader Abe Wharewaka commented 'business turns me on' (*Herald*, 15/11/86), was the one notably positive portrayal of gangs in the thousands of words written about them over a 10-year period. But it was instantly negated by the Ambury Park rape, and the hysteria generated over it in the media. It was a grave setback to the plans of the Auckland chapter to bring its members back into mainstream society — the 'credibility of the gang', according to the mayor of Manukau City, 'had been destroyed' (*Herald*, 15/12/86).

Meanwhile, in the South Island, the police declared open season on gangs with a 'Police Probe on Gang Work Schemes' (*Herald*, 15/10/86). Though the Labour Department, which administered the work schemes, had not lodged a complaint of impropriety, the schemes were described by a police officer in one press report as 'a pipeline to Treasury for the gangs' (*Herald*, 15/10/86). Contracts ranging from $90,000 up to $900,000 were said to have been siphoned off to the gangs. Although the Government's Project Employment Programme was designed for the unemployed, the money spent on the scheme was described in one report as '$4 Million Spent on Gang Jobs' (*Sunday Times*, 25/1/87). The accretion of Mafia-like status to gangs by slanted news reports was hardly negated by the police censure of the commander of the Invercargill police district for leaking an incomplete report on the work schemes to the press (*Herald*, 13/3/87).

Because of the longstanding negative media image of gangs, gang-bashing can be indulged in by politicians, police, local bodies and newspapers without fear of contradiction. Although there are only an estimated 2000 Maori gang members throughout New Zealand, the continuous negative coverage of their activities by the press is felt as an embarrassment by the other 400000 law-abiding Maori. The long-running denigration and criticism of gangs is a constant reproach to Maori society while providing sensational copy for newspapers. In other words, gang-bashing in the media is a socially acceptable albeit oblique form of Maori-bashing. Pakeha gangs such as Highway 61 and Hell's Angels do not come in for the same attention.

The Maori loans affair[1]

While the anti-social behaviour of Maori gangs was given extensive media coverage, conservative Maori leaders were also likely to come in for a bashing even when pursuing laudable social goals. The so-called 'Maori loans affair' is a case in point. The 1984 Hui Taumata (summit conference) of Maori leaders recommended the establishment of a Maori Development Bank to assist Maori economic development. Consequently the Secretary of Maori Affairs, Dr Tamati Reedy, entered into negotiations for an offshore loan of $600 million at the discount interest rate of 6 percent. Dr Reedy was not empowered to authorise such a loan. The Minister of Finance, who was, put a stop to the loan negotiations under advice from Treasury on 24 November 1987. Nevertheless the 'Maori loans affair' remained a hot issue in the media for over two months.

The media speculated on the likely source of the loan funds and whether they involved Arab money or 'Marcos millions' (*Star*, 17/12/86, *Herald*, 18/12/86). A parallel was drawn by the *Herald* with an 'earlier scandal' that 'blotted the career' of Sir Apirana Ngata (18/12/86). Other stories told of 'New Zealand Loan Emissaries' being 'Two Former Bankrupts' (*Sunday Star*, 21/12/86) and a 'Key Maori Loans Man Who Ran Broke Companies' (*Auckland Star*, 18/12/86). A *Herald* editorial warned that Maoridom had a 'Taniwha by the Tail' (18/12/86). Two years later, when Pakeha investment companies lost millions of real dollars of investors' money in the wake of the sharemarket crash, recriminations were relatively muted.

Maori people were shell-shocked by the unprecedented level of media Maori-bashing generated by the affair as headline followed headline — 'Maori Affairs in for Shakeup Come What May' (*Herald*, 19/12/86); 'Report on Loan Is White-wash Say Nat MPs' (*Star*, 18/12/86); 'Maori Leaders Knew of the Loans Affair' (*Herald*, 19/12/86); 'PM Calls on Mr Wetere to Explain' (*Herald*, 6/7/87); 'Maori Loan Row Not Finished With Yet' (*Herald*, 10/2/87); 'Inquiry the Only Way Out' (*Star*, 10/2/87).

Two months earlier the Deane report to Parliament had made it clear that the Finance Minister had stopped the loan, yet the press persisted. The affair had taken on a life of its own. Even when the Speaker of the House ruled in a breach of privilege case that Mr Wetere had not misled the House over the issue, and 'closed the lid' on the Peters–Wetere feud (*Star*, 11/2/87), the media were reluctant to release their hapless victim.

Ten months later, the *Herald* ran a story headlined 'Second Maori Loan Affair Looming' (9/12/87). The *Star* also attempted to resurrect the moribund theme with the story of the Audit Office's inquiry into what became known as 'the second Maori loans affair' (*Star*, 11/12/87).

This protracted fixation of the press with a loan that never occurred is explicable on two grounds: first, the commercial importance of sensational news in order to maintain market share in the newspaper business; secondly, the preservation of the structural relationship of Pakeha dominance and Maori subordination. Maori financial independence posed a serious challenge to that relationship.

The Waitangi Tribunal

Since 1985, when the Waitangi Tribunal was authorised to hear claims retrospective to 1840, Maori leaders have taken a number of steps aimed at redressing past injustices arising out of colonisation. There are now more than 150 claims before the Tribunal, the two most important being the Ngai Tahu claim for the 'tenths' in the South Island[2] and the Tainui claim for the million acres confiscated for military settlers. These claims have aroused deep-rooted fears of Pakeha dispossession, fears that were exacerbated in 1987 when the High Court granted the Maori Council's injunction claiming that the transfer of crown lands to state-owned enterprises prejudiced claims before the Waitangi Tribunal. The five judges were unanimous that the Treaty of Waitangi overrode the State Owned Enterprises Act.

Then, in October 1987, another injunction granted by Judge Greig recognised the Maori right to fisheries under the Treaty of Waitangi by suspending the Government's Individual Transferable Quota (ITQ) fisheries management regime. The Maori challenge for the return of their resources was now conducted on two fronts — land and sea. These initiatives to reverse the Pakeha monopoly on resources on the basis of treaty rights have inevitably resulted in heightened racial tension.

Maori people have felt the pain of dispossession under the Treaty of Waitangi for 150 years. But before even one acre of land was returned to the Maori, or one cent of compensation paid, by the Waitangi Tribunal the views of Pakeha crying foul were given prominence in newspapers. 'That Treaty? — Scrap It and Substitute Another Pact' argued Ralph Maxwell, Under-Secretary for Agriculture and Fisheries (*Herald*, 25/1/88). The Leader of the Opposition thought claims before the Waitangi Tribunal were starting 'to gnaw away at [Pakeha] New Zealanders' (*Herald*, 4/12/87). Mr Bolger suspected 'Bias in Tribunal' (*Herald*, 13/2/88).

Fear of Maori winning back some of their stolen resources through the courts or the Waitangi Tribunal was readily translated by politicians such as Sir Robert Muldoon into 'Race Relations Fear' (*Sunday Star*, 20/3/88). Although 'Racist Solutions' were 'Rejected by Party Leader' Mr Bolger (*Herald*, 6/8/88), 'Race Issues' returned to 'Haunt Parties' (*Herald*, 13/8/88) on the occasion of the National Party Conference. The views of the Member for Tauranga, Winston Peters, that the Treaty of Waitangi was outmoded and needed review, and that the National Party would target the Tribunal as an 'instrument of possible injustice to Pakehas', reflected Pakeha feelings. These views, expressed on behalf of his Pakeha constituents, alienated Mr Peters from his Maori colleagues in the party.

Conclusion

In 1988, the news media dwelt at length on the issue of race relations. But the subject was treated in a sensationalist way that emphasised, even fomented, racial antagonism, as exemplified by the 'kill a white' row. Little weight was given to the economic and social context — unemployment and competition for jobs and resources, which hurt Maori in particular. The end effect was the creation of a racist backlash which enabled politicians to counter successfully the challenge to Pakeha dominance. Since the challenge was made before the Waitangi Tribunal, public perceptions, led by the media debate, turned against the Tribunal itself. The Treaty of Waitangi and the Tribunal, key political issues in 1990, have already been publicly branded.

The conclusion drawn is that in any contest between Maori and Pakeha over land, resources or cultural space, media coverage functions, unwittingly or otherwise, to maintain Pakeha dominance. The Fourth Estate is controlled by Pakeha.

It selects the events it deems newsworthy, which usually centre on violence, conflict and competition. When these events involve Maori and Pakeha, it consistently represents the Pakeha status quo, helping them to maintain their power. So long as this unequal power relationship persists, the struggle of the Maori for a just and equitable society is a struggle without end.

Chapter 4

NEW ZEALAND JOURNALISTS: ONLY PARTLY PROFESSIONAL

Gary Wilson

You can trace a lot of lop-sided journalism back to the deprived childhood of New Zealand's journalists. Ten percent of them come from overseas, mostly the United Kingdom, so they haven't been taught much of our history or the Maori language when they were at school. That was no barrier, though, to becoming a New Zealand journalist, and once they got work in the media here, they were automatically licensed to explain New Zealand to New Zealanders. Never mind the gaps in their knowledge. They probably couldn't count to five in Maori. Never been on a marae. Couldn't say korero, let alone have one. No idea who Kawiti was or Te Whiti or Te Puea. And not at all sure what to make of the Treaty of Waitangi.

All that ignorance is quite a handicap when you're in the news business. But immigrant journalists don't have a monopoly on ignorance. That's shared by most of the journalists who went to school in New Zealand. Our schools have practically specialised in keeping kids clueless about their background.

We're a step ahead of the immigrant journalists in some ways. We've absorbed words like hangi and tangi, kai and ka pai — we probably have a bigger Maori vocabulary than we realise. Also, our school days did give us an inkling about Kupe, Hone Heke and half a dozen other Maori figures from last century. And we might have learned *Po Kare Kare Ana* and a couple of lines from *Ka Mate Ka Mate*. But it's a lightweight legacy.

Products of that education system need remedial treatment if they're to understand their country. And the 'better' the school they went to, the more urgent the need. It's the 'good' schools whose educational training has been the most staunchly Pakeha.

The system, naturally, isn't keen to admit that it's wrong, and that it's been wrong all along. When Education Department officials faced the Waitangi Tribunal during the hearing on te reo Maori, they put on a brave face, described the efforts through the years to raise Maori educational attainment, and concluded: 'The record to date is mixed.' The Waitangi Tribunal heard them out but saw it differently: 'We think the record to date is quite unmixed. It is a dismal failure and no amount of delicate phrasing can mask that fact.'[1] The Tribunal recommended to the Minister of Education that there be an urgent inquiry into the way Maori language and culture is taught in the schools.

The Minister might also ask a few questions about history teaching — such as how come most kids are still going through high school without studying New Zealand history? Introducing an emphatically Kiwi syllabus for senior students is great for those who take history. But most senior students don't have to, so they don't. And the ignorance endures.

Of course, the damage is done to youngsters heading into every kind of career, not just those bound for journalism. It messes up each new crop of lawyers, labourers, teachers, office workers — whoever. But the effect on prospective journalists is especially serious because their blinkered view of society determines what the public sees and hears. If they've still got the twisted view of New Zealand that school gave them, then they'll tell twisted stories.

Perhaps the journalism training courses have been sorting all that out? Well, no. It would be comforting to think so, but they haven't managed that at all. Firstly, today's news executives came into the media when there was no journalism training. They were at school in the 1940s, '50s and '60s. Their experience has been simply to move from one system (education) where Maori had no place to another (the media) where the same was true.

Another reason for journalism training not solving the problem is that substantial numbers of recruits to the media have bypassed the courses. A survey by Geoff Lealand in 1988 indicated that 65 percent of our 3 000 journalists had no formal training.[2] That's partly because journalism training has a short history here. Full-time courses were launched in Wellington and Christchurch in the 1960s and in Auckland in 1973. Together they trained about 130 students a year, and still do. That rate never satisfied the appetite of the media, which picked up recruits wherever they could. And, even though another hundred passed through other courses in the late 1980s, the media still recruit untrained staff.

There's a more important reason, though, for the courses' failure to come up with a remedy. Until 1985 none of them tried. And they didn't try because they didn't see a problem.

The most influential courses are the three oldest — those at the University of Canterbury, Wellington Polytechnic and Auckland Technical Institute. The Canterbury course is a year-long postgraduate programme that provided little practical training until Brian Priestley took over in the mid-1970s. But Wellington and ATI were different. They took anyone, from school-leavers to graduates, and they zeroed in on practical, marketable skills. Geoff Black at ATI was especially astute in gauging what the industry wanted and how to shape the students for that world.

Not too surprisingly, the industry didn't see any problem in hiring recruits whose heritage and training were exclusively Pakeha. So the courses reflected that indifference. Occasionally, a Maori or Pacific Island student would train at ATI or Wellington Polytechnic. (Among them were Philip Whaanga, Mata Mihinui, Fraser Folster, Morehu McDonald and Mamae Wikiriwhi.) But they and their classmates all toed a Pakeha line because there was only one language and news was judged, gathered and written according to Pakeha rules.

So training hasn't provided the answer. Not yet anyway. Still, there has been a change since 1980. That year, the Journalists' Training Board and the Department of Maori Affairs began a series of five-day introductory courses for Maori and Pacific Island students. The programme was based on the notion that New Zealand journalism would be the better for a strong Maori and Pacific Island presence. A survey that year suggested that Maori and Pacific Island journalists amounted to less than 2 percent of the total.

Those dip and dabble courses tapped into talent straight away. Within a couple of years, more than a score of bright prospects were either already working in the media or heading that way. Tapu Misa trained at Wellington Polytechnic and soon gained a national reputation as a feature writer. Suzanne Tichborne went from ATI into newspaper work and surfaced as editor of a community newspaper. Rawiri Wright, who'd been a teacher, embarked on a circuit that took in ATI, the *Taranaki Herald*, the *Evening Post*, and then journalism tutoring. Sef Hao'uli went from ATI to the *Sunday News*, to the Prime Minister's Department as a press secretary, back to the *Sunday News*, on to TVNZ and then into his own communications company.

Within six years, the courses had propelled more than 70 Maori and Pacific Island students into newspaper, radio and television journalism. Wellington Polytechnic and ATI couldn't accommodate that flow, although they did accept more Maori and Pacific Island students, and gave a little more attention to Maori issues. But the selection criteria and the curriculum didn't change much. So in 1985, Waiariki Polytechnic (then a community college) set up a full-time, six-month course which aimed to cover what the others did and, in addition, focused on Maoritanga. The selection criteria were almost identical. Waiariki, like the other courses, wanted students who were keen on journalism, with a good command of English, an impressive academic record, above average intelligence, a wide range of interests, and who were well informed, mature, personable, reliable, presentable and energetic.

But Waiariki also wanted students strong in, or committed to, Maoritanga. At Manukau Polytechnic, the following year, there was a similar course established to train Pacific Island journalists. And over the next few years, courses got under way at Christchurch Polytechnic (where the emphasis was on broadcasting), Northland Polytechnic in Whangarei, and Aoraki Polytechnic in Timaru. From the outset, the new courses edged away from the strictly Pakeha style that had been the pattern in the media. These developments have encouraged the three old courses to broaden their approach too. Though their response has so far been tentative and inadequate, it's a start.

The country's newsrooms have also made a start. They needed to. The media haven't been at their best when it comes to Maori news. In fact, there's nothing they handle quite so badly — unless it's Pacific Island stories. They bungle Maori news in all sorts of ways — playing down big issues (such as Maori language teaching); missing the Maori implications in other issues (such as immigration); ignoring stories completely (such as any number of major hui or festivals); quoting people who aren't Maori authorities (such as Winston Peters or Bob Jones) and neglecting those who are; blowing up negative stories (such as the Hana Te Hemara remarks), and getting them wrong (as with Hana), then denying they got them wrong (Hana again).

You could say that all that adds up to Maori bashing. It's not such a bad term. It *is* bashing. And it's the Maori who are being bashed. The only trouble is the phrase suggests that it's all on purpose, which isn't true. Maori bashing is like bad breath — avoidable, unpleasant, but unintentional. The significant difference is that Maori bashing does real lasting damage as well as causing offence. Radio and television add insult to injury — they mispronounce too: and they've been doing it from the beginning. Let's take three examples:

Radio New Zealand's chief parliamentary reporter, Richard Griffin, is articulate and authoritative about what goes on around the Beehive — and yet he's consistently wrong with four out of Koro Wetere's five syllables.

Keith Quinn, the best informed of TVNZ's sports team, can always correctly pronounce the names of the Maori footballers — but only if they've been conveniently christened Bill Bush or Wayne Shelford or the like. Pokere, Tuoro, Nepia, Herewini and others regularly receive unsolicited vowel transplants.

Ian Cross, former boss of the BCNZ, takes pride in the development of the TV programmes *Te Karere* and *Koha* — yet can pronounce neither.

A handful of broadcasters, though, are handling Maori confidently and accurately. It's music to the ear, and about time too. Any other encouraging signs? Yes, there are a few:

- Pakeha journalists in growing numbers aren't comfortable with the way the media are operating and are working for change — lending a hand at Waiariki and Manukau, helping young Maori and Pacific Island journalists, questioning ingrained newsroom routines, and trying to avoid the reflex actions of conventional Pakeha journalists.
- A growing body of new material — such as *The Treaty of Waitangi* by Claudia Orange and *The New Zealand Wars* by James Belich — is shedding fresh light on New Zealand history.
- Maori and Pacific Island journalists are gaining the experience and seniority to challenge Pakeha views on news and current affairs.
- There have been various moves towards independent professional Maori and Pacific Island news organisations and publications.
- Growing numbers of young journalists, especially students, are wanting to learn taha Maori. That easily topped the list of subjects needing more emphasis during training, according to course graduates in the 1988 survey. It was also well up on the list of refresher training priorities for working journalists in the same survey.

All this is positive but it doesn't have the force to make the media clean up their act at all quickly. If professionalism is wanted promptly, something like a revolution is needed. It would be especially helpful if media executives were to take stock of what they know about New Zealand society. And if they don't know much about the non-Pakeha elements then they should acknowledge that ignorance. There's no need for fits of guilt. But if they're ignorant about a lot of the people whose views and concerns they're being paid to reflect and serve, then they should face that. Next they might mull over the implications of this ignorance. For instance, it probably means that overall they're doing a lousy job, and they should face that. Once they can recognise their shortcomings and those of their profession, they might be prepared to become more professional.

That process may require examining a few conventional assumptions about news. One such assumption is that news organisations have been reasonably objective all along. Like other media critics, Philip Tremewan isn't convinced.[3]

> Objectivity is an important Pakeha media myth. Ritual references are often made to it and it's an underlying article of faith for many journalists.
>
> It is, like many articles of faith, a contradiction in its own terms. It assumes journalists work either like an omniscient deity or else are able to shed their limited knowledge and approach each story with a tabula rasa.
>
> In fact, Pakeha journalists decide what is and isn't news according to their own cultural definitions, they choose the angle, they choose who to talk to out of their limited range of contacts (who often include no Maori at all) and the outcome is inevitably racist.
>
> It's like the judicial system which has a similar impartiality myth, but again the outcome has been clearly documented as racist with widely different treatment meted out to Maori and Pakeha.

Other assumptions which deserve querying include:

- That the lapses in Maori and Pacific Island news are occasional, usually minor and no more serious than the failings in other rounds (when all evidence suggests that the lapses are daily, frequently major, and the consequences profound).
- That activists are pushing for special treatment and are demanding only favourable publicity (when the call is simply for a fair go).
- That separate courses and independent publications and news organisations are separatist, unnecessary and unwelcome (when experience shows that dependence doesn't work).
- That reasonable solutions would be found if Maori negotiators would only be calm and patient (and compliant and not too uppity?).
- That we should let bygones be bygones, ignore talk of back rent and concentrate on co-operation (which is not a bad argument when you've run up a big debt).
- That encouraging Maori and Pacific Island recruits will lower the standards of journalism (when the standards have been held down by an oversupply of Pakeha journalists with a narrow range of knowledge).
- That if the Maori want better coverage they should see that the media are kept informed. (Too right. But that doesn't let the media off the hook — they're the ones with the newshounds.)

Media executives and their journalists should chew over these matters. They could then move on to look to a plan of action to help put things right. Such a plan could include six steps:

1. Retraining all staff so that they're capable of treating non-Pakeha New Zealanders as professionally as the others. That won't be easy or cheap, but justice can be difficult and costly to achieve.
2. Hiring only those recruits who have the capacity to be New Zealand professionals. Our media need to be more choosy.

3. Seeking advice, if need be, outside the usual news team for ideas on non-Pakeha stories.
4. Buying stories and programmes from Maori and Pacific Island agencies if the home team can't deliver.
5. Leaning on the training courses until they routinely produce graduates who can handle non-Pakeha as well as Pakeha stories.
6. Making a fuss until our schools teach what New Zealand youngsters need in order to be New Zealanders — that means Maoritanga and New Zealand history for everyone.

Maori and Pacific Island leaders shouldn't be passive either. They need to recognise, as too few have done so far, that the media have a huge influence on the welfare of their people. Uninformed media produce a misinformed public — and that'll block progress anywhere. So the media must be a top priority in any development strategy.

And then they should recognise that a strong Maori and Pacific Island presence won't be established in the media unless that's planned and co-ordinated and built around professionals who are up to the task. Developments so far have been piecemeal. Perhaps the Ministries of Maori Affairs and Pacific Island Affairs can take the initiative. We all lose if someone doesn't.

Chapter 5
RACE-TAGGING: THE MISUSE OF LABELS AND THE PRESS COUNCIL
Bernard Kernot

The unnecessary use of racial or ethnic references of the type referred to as race-labelling or race-tagging is a well-established practice in New Zealand newspapers. Back in the 1950s, Richard Thompson, a Canterbury University sociologist, drew attention to it in an analysis of press handling of Maori news. He concluded that 'the practice of race-labelling Maori crime news was widespread, unjustified, and inasmuch as the practice was virtually limited in its use to the Maori people, discriminatory'.[1]

In more recent years, Race Relations Conciliators have expressed their unease at the way the media present news which touches on racial and ethnic matters. The late Harry Dansey, himself a newspaper journalist before becoming our second Race Relations Conciliator, raised the point of the negative presentation of minority groups in a review of media responsibility in his 1977 Report. He observed that 'news showing [minority groups] in a poor light is accentuated, but stories showing them in a positive or good light are played down or not published at all'.[2] As if to confirm the point, Wellington's *Evening Post* recently featured prominently a court report on Peter Andrian, described as this country's most accomplished burglar. The judge's comments that Andrian was a Czechoslovak refugee who received New Zealand citizenship and subsequently embarked on a life of crime were fully reported. Immediately above this story, the *Post* featured a photograph of the recipients of this country's highest award, the Order of New Zealand. Among those honoured was Mr Fred Turnovsky. Neither in the caption, nor in a later news item, was there any mention of Mr Turnovsky's Czechoslovak origins (*Evening Post*, 12/8/88, 15/8/88).

My own concern at the prevalence in newspapers of race-tagging in crime and court reports led me to make inquiries with the New Zealand Press Council early in 1986. I asked how the reporting of racial and ethnic details was covered in the code of ethics I presumed the Council held. The response was surprising. The matter had never been considered by the Council, and it had no clear position on the issue. At my request, I was invited to make a written submission and discuss it with the Council.

In preparing the submission, I undertook a month-long survey of crime reports appearing in Wellington's two dailies. The survey produced six examples of irrelevant race-tagging. In each case, the tag was applied gratuitously where other ethnic clues were missing; they added nothing to the newsworthiness of the reports;

none was applied to Pakeha (or Europeans or Caucasians); and the tagging served no public interest. For example, one report stated: 'Police are seeking a Maori man, 43, whose identity is known, in connection with the stabbing . . .' (*Dominion*, 20/2/86). This is not a description for a wanted man since the police already know the identity of the suspect. The 'Maori' tag adds nothing to the newsworthiness of the report.

The six examples illustrated how race-tagging was employed in addition to the simple case given above. There was, for instance, the use of the term 'part-Maori', as in the following report:

> Somewhere in Christchurch is a would-be rapist nursing sore private parts. . . . The Christchurch woman, 34, was walking home just after 12.30 p.m. when approached by a man naked from the waist down. The part-Maori leaped at the woman and tried to tear off her clothing. She grappled with him, then seized him by his unprotected genitals. He fled. A detective reported that from her account of the incident, the attacker was likely to be still in pain [*Evening Post*, 11/2/86].

The racial identification is clearly not part of a description of a wanted man. The tone of the report is more jocular than serious, but the use of the term 'part-Maori' is particularly reprehensible. Who decides which 'part' of a person of mixed heritage gets tagged? I invited the Council to examine the logic of the term and rule against its use.

Another story referred to Andy Narain as 'the New Zealand-born Indian faith healer' (*Evening Post*, 28/1/86, 29/1/86, *Dominion*, 12/2/86), a term that is as misleading as it is prejudicial. There is an implication that Narain is not a New Zealander after all. When do people of Indian heritage qualify as New Zealanders?

The submission referred in detail to these examples because they demonstrated that irrelevant race-tagging in crime reporting occurred regularly, that it was selective in targeting minorities, and that it accentuated their negative aspects.

When I discussed it with the Council in May 1986, the chairman, Sir Thaddeus McCarthy, made it clear that the issue raised in the submission was totally new to the Council, and that it would need time to consider it.

Some weeks later, I was advised of the Council's decision to send a guidance note to all editors. In it, the Council outlined my case, and accepted the 'fundamental point that racial origins should not be referred to in reports of court cases or concerning wanted persons unless that feature is plainly relevant'.[3] It also noted that there were 'more frequent references to racial origins than on the face of things seems necessary'.[4]

Having established that the submission had merit, the note went on to review the house rules of metropolitan dailies and found that most of them already had rules that covered the point. The real problem it disclosed was the widespread failure of editors to observe their own house rules where matters of race were concerned. From the public interest point of view, this is alarming and confirms the suspicion of many people that the press does not address racial issues responsibly. Yet despite this revelation, the note merely 'invited' editors to avoid irrelevant racial references. In other words, the Council declined to do more than pass on my 'plea' to errant editors.

Not surprisingly, the guidance note has had minimal impact. This is illustrated by a letter that appeared in the *Evening Post* (2/3/88) complaining about the use of the label 'part-Maori' in a prominent front-page crime report. After pointing out that a part-Maori had to be a part something else, the correspondent asks, 'So why the Maori tag? Does it add to the news item to identify any race at all?' These were questions I had raised two years earlier and which the guidance note was meant to settle.

While the Council failed to act decisively towards its own members, it also failed to act in the best public interest when it did not release a press statement of its findings and adjudication, as is its normal practice. The public, and especially those most affected by race-tagging, have not been informed of the Council's attitude, and are thereby deprived of the opportunity to bring complaints based on well-defined ethical principles. Why the Council chose not to issue a statement was never explained to me, but by keeping a public silence on the matter, the Council leaves itself open to the charge of shielding those editors whose unethical practices deserve to be exposed.

Three points emerge from the above discussion. The first is the relatively low priority the Council appears to give to matters of broad public interest, as distinct from the more narrowly defined interests of the newspaper industry. The most glaring example of this is the fact that it had not considered the problem of race-tagging and other manifestations of racism in the press, despite a history of complaints, often from authoritative sources. Its reluctance to take the public into its confidence in the present case is another example. Racism poses ethical problems which the press must address in the public interest, and the Council needs to show a greater sensitivity and openness to public concerns.

Secondly, the Council appears to lack the necessary 'teeth' to make it an effective watchdog of the industry's ethics. Guidance notes are not binding on editors even in matters of serious ethical concern.

Finally, it is the writer's view that the Press Council, rather than the Race Relations Office, should take primary responsibility for disciplining editors and newspapers for breaches of ethics relating to racism. Perhaps the time has come for the Press Council to review its functions, role, representation and authority so as to become an effective watchdog on behalf of both the public interest and the interests of the newspaper industry.

II

THE MEDIUM
&
THE MESSAGE

HAVING DISCUSSED GENERAL issues in Part I, the following section addresses specific aspects of the mass media.

Philip Whaanga begins by providing an insight into the world of radio, and identifying areas of neglect and insensitivity when it comes to coverage of issues of interest and concern to Maori. Tribal radio is one option if some of these inadequacies are to be addressed, and this issue is taken up again in Part III. Geoff Lealand discusses that most powerful of media: television. The key point he makes is that New Zealand television is dominated by overseas content, so that we are much more likely to see American race relations than our own portrayed in drama or comedy programmes. How are we to understand our own cultural heritage or matters of contemporary political importance if they are largely excluded from our television screens?

Radio provides more options than television, and two are discussed in the following chapters. Lesley Max discusses the potential of talk-back radio to provide a forum for discussion of race relations and then shows why it has failed to realise that potential. Peter Tohill is more optimistic about access radio, and sees it as a means of providing a direct link with, and between, ethnic communities unhampered by mainstream media controls.

Andrew Trlin examines how the *Dominion* uses its editorials and letters to the editor columns to encourage a positive debate about race relations. He argues that the *Dominion*'s approach provides something of a model for other newspapers. Finally, Stephenie Knight surveys recent coverage by overseas media of New Zealand's race relations. Our international image has always embraced singular perceptions of the nature of local intergroup relations. Among recent reports, some are appallingly crude and alarmist; others, though still critical, are more balanced.

Chapter 6

RADIO: CAPABLE OF CARRYING A BICULTURAL MESSAGE?

Philip Whaanga

The two worlds of the Pakeha and the Maori seem to be on a collision course, and contradictory messages from the message carriers are not helping.

The Pakeha message is carried by the mainstream media. These channels are distinguished from their Maori counterpart by being better resourced and carrying the stamp of the majority culture. For the Maori world, the message is still spread mainly by word of mouth and, like the culture, has an 'underground' and unofficial status. Because early colonising efforts focused on the civilising effect of the written word, the spoken word came to have a lower priority. The arrival of radio did little to alter the impact of these new priorities on the Maori world.

Yet radio coverage of the signing of the Treaty of Waitangi might have conveyed a totally different meaning from that which has come down to us through five English language treaty versions and a revised Maori translation of the missing English first draft.

Radio would have captured the initial ambiguity and misunderstanding on which modern New Zealand was founded. Of course, that's presuming that the state-owned enterprise Radio New Zealand Ltd could have afforded an outside broadcast, or that tribal radio could have raised enough money to stay on air to cover the treaty hui. Or that private radio succeeded in getting Maori Council sponsorship to bring you selected highlights.

But perhaps this is all a little flippant, because radio, in whatever hands, follows some rules. It is only now, after a century and a half, that Maori are making their voices heard on the airwaves and challenging some of these rules. The following discussion looks at how radio has been used to tell us who we are as New Zealanders.

The medium of radio

Radio reporting relies on people with the skill to summarise what is being discussed. A clear, lively speaking voice is essential for both interviewer and interviewee. Those who use lots of big words and take a long time to make a point do not communicate well on radio.

News broadcasts on radio have severe time restrictions, giving out a little information at a time, in hourly or half-hourly bulletins. A picture is built up by allowing an initial statement and then seeking comment to throw light on it. Sometimes, if the story is initially uncovered by a different branch of the media, the original statement may be downplayed, with the focus on the reaction. The original speaker may then be asked to comment on the comment.

Radio has a target audience which peaks at breakfast time, so a good story is sometimes saved until then. If interested parties cannot be found to comment, the reporters themselves will need to. Reporters pride themselves on their impartiality and professionalism, yet in an imperfect radio world the biases are often reflected simply in the choice of opinions sought.

Radio current affairs programmes provide the opportunity for analysis of news developments over a period of time. Private radio has pioneered 'newstalk', a sort of news commentary on the cheap, but the upshot of this development has been the cultivation of highly opinionated broadcasters. With newstalk, the private radio stations, with such hosts as Gordon Dryden and Tim Bickerstaff, stole a march on their state-funded cousins George Balani and current media doyen Paul Holmes.

Radio reporting is of course vulnerable to bias and error. Misinformation, either from a wrong interpretation by the reporter, or through unreliable informants, can become accepted as fact simply through repetition. At times, radio reportage is compromised by the sheer mechanics of getting the news out 'first, fast and factual'.

Because of the speed and urgency involved, with shorter deadlines in which to gather and present news stories, radio attracts younger staff. The general format of most radio stations reinforces this youthful image. State radio, once the preserve of 'Aunty BBC' clones, is having to come to terms with this commercial thrust as a state-owned enterprise. So most radio journalists are young, mobile and lack life experience; and all but a handful are Pakeha, with Pakeha ideas of what a news story should sound like.

In a recent survey of editors and chief reporters, senior news management in print and radio acknowledged their poor understanding of tikanga Maori, but judged themselves competent to evaluate the newsworthiness of Maori issues. In a country whose indigenous people are found in nearly all walks of life, a country founded on a bicultural agreement, the media continue to perform a major disservice to all New Zealanders, for they have neglected to tell the biggest story of all: who we are.

Processes and values

In the largely 'underground' Maori world, important discussion still takes place on rural marae, in homes and in the workplace. Because important and skilled people in the Maori world are not necessarily holding down important positions in the Pakeha world (they may be gang leaders or kohanga reo kaitiaki), meetings are held out of work time so they can attend. Thus, weekend hui are commonplace. But that is just the time when reporters are scarce because of weekend penal pay rates, so most important hui are simply not reported. Perhaps the reporter needs to seek an on-the-spot explanation. But it is not enough to pay a quick visit, or just phone someone up to find out what happened. Even when Pakeha reporters *are* available, their ignorance of Maoritanga usually means a wealth of interesting information remains uncovered.

Certainly time constraints also restrict reporting in other areas, such as finance and education, but these sectors have alternative avenues of information dissemination available and professional advocates to promote their message. The Maori world still relies largely on the hui process of word of mouth and photocopied newsletters, and as a result has been largely shut out by the media.

News selection in radio, as in print and television, is almost exclusively in the hands of monocultural, monolingual males. While much more attention has been recently focused on things Maori in the media, it adds up to little of substance.

When the Department of Maori Affairs, through Koro Wetere and former Prime Minister David Lange, announced its devolution proposals, the same monocultural and monolingual journalists covered the familiar ground. One Radio New Zealand journalist produced an edited recording of the two ministers' fumbling explanations rather than seeking tribal comment on what devolving power-sharing to iwi meant.

Expectations of Maori ineptitude and lack of sophistication are sometimes reinforced by Maori bureaucratic bungling. From a steady diet of media messages, we have learned that Maori Access schemes are just used to rip off the system and that dark deals among Maoridom persist until Winston comes along to expose them. But few journalists have done their homework and are sufficiently informed to make more than value judgements. That Koro Wetere has difficulty in explaining things is not helped by reporters with listening impairments, and those who have decided that Winston Peters sounds better. Peters has mastered the main radio news requirement of speaking in 30-second clips, essential to quick, easy editing. But Peters was elected by voters on a Pakeha electoral roll, while Wetere was elected solely on the Western Maori ticket. It may be of value for journalists to consider this distinction when comparing the credibility of the two.

Radio reporting is by its nature skimpy. Most news broadcasts cannot provide the full picture, let alone analysis. The listener is left with impressions which tend to emphasise the sensational.

Radio and cultural misunderstanding

Here are two examples of cultural misunderstandings that in themselves were not past rectifying, yet pride and stubbornness blocked solutions. The first is a news item from Radio New Zealand's 2ZB.

> A Wellington lawyer told the district court today it was pointless for him to ask for suppression of his client's name as, in what he described as the worst traditions of the press, his name, and what amounted to a summary of facts and a victim impact report from the alleged assault incident, had already received wide publicity before the charged man appeared in court.
>
> Lawyer Peter Boshier was appearing for Prison Officer Koro Tainui Wetere, 26-year-old son of the Minister of Maori Affairs, who appeared on a charge of assaulting a female.
>
> The charge arose from an alleged incident at Arohata Women's Prison in which a woman prisoner was allegedly assaulted. . . . Wetere has denied the charge and is to face a defended hearing at the beginning of next month.
>
> Mr Boshier told the court that the publication of Wetere's name before his

court appearance had been an affront to the judge he was appearing before, and had usurped the function of the court. . . . Judge Carolyn Henwood said the court was disturbed by the publicity, and agreed with Mr Boshier that because of it, an early hearing of the charge was required.

This Radio New Zealand story may look relatively innocuous. Yet a news story had been run throughout the morning of the previous Tuesday, describing how the Minister of Maori Affairs' son was to be charged with assault. So the newspapers did it too; that is no defence. Perhaps the writer of Friday's court story didn't know about the earlier coverage. RNZ received a complaint before the Friday story, but perhaps not quick enough for RNZ management to act on. The complaint, by the Secretary of the New Zealand Maori Council, Mr Tata Parata, related to several matters, including:

• The identification of the defendant by name and his relationship to the Minister, along with the charge he was to face;
• Steps taken by the police to obtain evidence (taking photographs of the complainant);
• The revelation that Wetere had been a prison warder for only nine days prior to the assault.

Mr Parata pointed out that the identification of Mr Wetere pre-empted his option for name suppression, and highlighted particular evidence (police photographs) which precluded his presenting evidence of his own.

> The publication of Mr Wetere's name is grossly prejudicial to his having a fair hearing. It was announced before he appeared in the District Court. The comment has been made that if he was the relative of a well-known non-Maori personality the news media would not have dared or bothered to comment on the event as they have in this case. It appears that radio news have willingly relaxed the constraints which others enjoy to ridicule the Minister of Maori Affairs. The racial implications speak for themselves.

The allegations that the story was run because he was the Minister's son were denied by RNZ news management. Later, Wetere junior was discharged, but that event did not, of course, raise the same media interest.

The other example concerns media treatment of the subject of death. A Maori woman died just before entering hospital for surgery for her weight problem. By news selection criteria, this story merits attention because it is unusual and arouses sympathy. It came to the attention of journalists through their regular contact with police, fire and ambulance services. A police sergeant told a reporter that it had taken several officers to carry a dead woman out of a house.

Regional News 2YA, 7.30 p.m. 23 September 1987
Announcer: A 343-kilogram woman died in . . . this morning, hours before she was due to go into hospital for treatment for her weight problem. Police say the 31-year-old woman travelled down from . . . over the last few days with her family for the treatment, and they had arranged for the Fire Service to get her to hospital today. She had apparently been confined to bed for several months because of her condition. It took five constables and two attendants to move the woman's

body out of the . . . house this morning. The woman weighed 54 stone, the equivalent of about five grown men.

A call to the relatives to check for details brought further elaboration to the story the next morning.

Morning Report 2YA, 24 September 1987
Announcer: The family of a woman believed to have been New Zealand's heaviest says she had been heartened by a letter of encouragement from Prime Minister David Lange.

The 343-kilo . . . woman who died yesterday wrote to Mr Lange several years ago to ask about his weight-reducing surgery. The dead woman's cousin says the prime ministerial reply was sensitive and supportive, while warning of the operation's risks.

Reporter: The 31-year-old woman named . . . died at her sister's home in . . . yesterday morning. She was single and lived on her own in . . ., but had been brought down to . . . last week. Her sister had been visiting up north and was worried about . . .'s health. Her cousin . . . told *Morning Report* that . . . had been extremely large from about the time she started school. She had been on numerous diets, and in and out of hospital over the years since then, but . . . says her cousin had a marvellous disposition, and never let herself get upset by the odd bit of teasing from local children. She says there was never much of that anyhow, as . . . was a favourite with kids at the local school where she worked part time as a librarian. . . . says . . . had many friends and socialised regularly, never missing a party, and was a regular at the local pub for a short while most days. She says that a weight well over 50 stone never seemed to get . . . down, and friends and family found her optimism inspiring.

A close relative of the woman came to see me about what he saw as insensitive reporting. I told him to put his complaint in writing. He did this, in Maori, and addressed it to the Director-General, Beverley Wakem. She, in turn, asked for a translation from RNZ's Haare Williams. I believe (as did the translator) that the writer conveyed, in Maori, deep hurt and puzzlement as to why his whanaunga should be treated as an object of curiosity. The writer also spoke of the inability of the relatives at the time of the tangihanga to answer the slurs to the memory of their loved one.

Acting General Manager of News Ray Lilley replied with an apology for any distress caused. But it was a case of Pakeha judgements of what makes news conflicting with the sensitivities of Maoritanga. As a professional journalist, he could not censure the authors of the news reports because the circumstances of the death were, at face value, so unusual that reporting could not be ignored. Mr Lilley supplied a copy of the longer item run on *Morning Report* to show the considerable efforts made to be as sensitive as possible. As a result of the complaint, he said, he was drawing to the attention of journalists the issue of personal and cultural sensitivity for both Maori and Pakeha. While he could not promise that RNZ would become perfect overnight in representing Maori matters, he hoped there would be acceptance that they were trying to improve understanding and reporting standards, and that where RNZ had Maori staff or people with a good knowledge of Maoritanga, they would be consulted.

The news manager also sent a covering memo to staff with his reply and the translation. In it, he reiterated his approval of the stories broadcast because of the Pakeha news perspective. He asked staff to 'think twice' about the sensitivities of those involved and said it would be helpful with Maori coverage to consult RNZ Maori staff or those with a good knowledge of Maoritanga. He finished by saying that in no way, however, should legitimate news coverage be inhibited. The news manager here admits to a Pakeha news perspective, but does not accept the need to accommodate a Maori perspective, because that might block 'legitimate' news. But whose values are being used to judge the perspective and what is legitimate?

I have used these examples because they are unusual. People who bother to make official complaints are far fewer than those who moan but do nothing. Yet I work with these radio journalists, and I can say categorically that nothing in the system has changed. No journalists have asked Maori staff for advice, and similar stories have been broadcast since.

Michael King offers good advice on gathering Maori news sensitively in the Journalists' Training Board booklet *Kawe Korero*. All New Zealand journalists should read and follow it.

The history

The meeting of Maori and Pakeha culture in the 1800s proved that Maori could adapt to the new technology in order to communicate. The printing press not only brought the Lord's word to Aotearoa, but also the first Maori language newspaper, *Te Karere Maori*, in 1842, published by the forerunner of the Maori Affairs Department. The tradition continued intermittently until 1987, when its modern day successor, *Tu Tangata* magazine, closed. (I had been its editor.)

But the partnership of Maori and Pakeha in private media never took off. Newspapers, and later radio, commented on Maori life when it impacted on European affairs, and viewed Maori custom from the standpoint of an outside observer rather than as an element of the same society.

Maori language broadcasts on the New Zealand Broadcasting Service began in 1942 when Wiremu Parker, of Ngati Porou, read out the weekly lists of war dead on the YA network. This was expanded into a weekly Maori news broadcast on Sunday night. (Even that was too much for some listeners, as a browse through early copies of *Listener* letters to the editor reveals.) His was a sole effort and was given no resources or support, unlike the European news service. In later years there were Purewa Biddle and Bill Kerekere. The Labour Government tried to establish a Polynesian radio station in 1972, but procrastination by the then New Zealand Broadcasting Corporation left the appointed manager without resources, and the change of government in 1975 left the plan still-born.

In 1978, a private radio contender, Radio Manukau, presented plans to cater for the large Polynesian population in Auckland, and eventually secured a warrant based on less music, more news and information and talkback radio. Radio Pacific was born. Each night, a different Polynesian culture would host. This development spurred the NZBC to ask their underutilised manager to set up a radio unit catering for South Auckland's Polynesians. This he did, broadcasting daily news programmes in Maori, Samoan, Cook Islands Maori, Tongan, Niuean and Tokelauan, with weekly current affairs magazine programmes in each language. It was called *Te Reo o Aotearoa*. The programmes are still broadcast for half an hour daily on National Radio. But as Maori broadcaster Derek Fox pointed out in his summary for the Royal Commission on Social Policy (1988), Radio New Zealand broadcast less than an hour of Maori language a week in 1987, despite an overall total of tens of thousands of broadcast hours.

The present

News in English about Maori events has suffered an even worse fate: it has almost disappeared. *Te Reo o Aotearoa* has over recent years lost its senior Maori-speaking staff. Unfortunately, journalism skills have had a low priority for New Zealand's Maori news-gathering unit, fluency in Maori being the pre-eminent requirement.

Information concerning Maori developments broadcast in both Maori and English is of a low standard, as has long been known by Radio New Zealand management. Many Maori no longer listen. As one old kaumatua told me, 'I just listen at that early hour to find out who's died so the wife and I can go to the tangi. The language spoken is atrocious anyway.'

In 1988 senior Radio New Zealand executives were asked by the Royal Commission on Social Policy to detail plans to improve Maori programming. The following is an extract from Derek Fox's submission:

Proposal

The Board of the Corporation agreed, in October 1984, to a range of future priorities in respect of Maori and Pacific Island programming:

1. The establishment of 1YB in Auckland as a Maori and Pacific Island Access station, with emphasis to be on Maori content. Links would be established with 2YB in Wellington, or further elements of Maori programming would be initiated on 2YB, such as a Maori breakfast session.
2. The establishment of a new post of Maori Affairs reporter at Radio New Zealand Head Office News, with other Maori Affairs posts to follow.
3. The establishment of regular Maori news bulletins in English on commercial stations and regular bulletins in English on the National Programme.
4. The provision of Maori Language Week type capsules for commercial stations to be played throughout the year (not just in Maori Language Week).
5. The extension of Community Notice Board facilities on commercial stations to include notices of hui, tangi and other events of interest to Maoris.
6. The provision of one minute duration information commercials with revenue potential on Maori history, culture and personalities in collaboration with the Departments of Maori Affairs and Education.
7. The promotion of modern Maori music and musicians on commercial stations.
8. The adoption of a monitoring scheme for Maori recruits specifically directed at maintaining their bicultural differences until they reach positions of influence in Radio New Zealand, which would enable them to affect the prevailing culture.
9. Encouragement of Pakeha staff to become bicultural and bilingual, with Maori modules in all suitable courses and facilities for outside studies.

10. The encouragement of mental orientation, in all RNZ decisionmakers, towards consideration of the Maori point of view in projects. This is to be fundamental, not token, and in a way that Maori influence can be exerted on the final decision or programme.

Action

It reads well and must have sounded even better. However, what has eventuated from that impressive list in the intervening four years?

1. Nothing. That plan, or something very similar, was mooted in 1978 shortly after the development of the Maori unit in Auckland.
2. Nothing. No appointment has been made. In fact, there is not one Maori reporter, whether monolingual or bilingual, in the head office of Radio New Zealand News.
3. Once a week there is a Maori news roundup on the National Programme. But Pakeha people get their news every hour and even more regularly in peak times. Would Pakeha people call a news roundup once a week sufficient? We have hardly advanced from Wiremu Parker's Maori news box of the 1950s and 1960s.
4. No evidence of this as a consumer.
5. No evidence of this as a consumer.
6. No evidence of this as a consumer.
7. It must be deduced that Maori people should be grateful to hear Maori music played on the stations in which they are shareholders. Somehow it is seen as a privilege, not a right.
8. RNZ has informed the Royal Commission on Social Policy that it is having trouble recruiting and retaining Maori staff. Clearly this is not working — so nothing again.
9. After sixty years of radio broadcasting, the only bilingual Maori/English person in the entire executive management of the BCNZ is the General Manager of the yet to be established Maori Radio Network.
10. This illustrates the token nature of the BCNZ commitment to Maori broadcasting and is an indication of the low value placed on things Maori by the executive management of BCNZ and its components.[1]

Radio New Zealand has since that time hired a Maori affairs reporter for its head office news team, but an Auckland slot remains unfilled. It has lost its remaining Maori language programme producer to private Maori radio and has been looking for some years for someone to fill Wiremu Parker's original position. RNZ has two Maori speakers reading news — one in Whangarei, one in Auckland. And the BCNZ's only bilingual Maori/English executive transferred to Aotearoa Maori Radio as general manager, but has since resigned. Radio New Zealand Ltd says it is considering contracting in Maori media expertise.

It has become clearer, year by year, that those controlling and working in the media are prejudiced and unprofessional and will not admit it. As Gary Wilson, former executive training officer of the New Zealand Journalists' Training Board, puts it: 'A regular part of the media's message is that Maori does not matter, not much anyway, and only then when it intrudes on the Pakeha world.' So stories of gangs and loan scandals dwarf those about kohanga reo or Ratana hui.

Tribal radio

One result of all this has been that Maori have taken their own initiative to bring about change. Derek Fox worked to establish television news in Maori in 1983. Nga Kaiwhakapumau i te Reo, the Wellington Maori Language Board, pioneered private Maori language radio, also in 1983, with the first of many short-term broadcasts. Programming was amateur but gripping, the music mostly live or archival. Wellington Maori and Pakeha supporters soon wanted more than a two-day spin.

In 1987, Te Upoko o te Ika Radio took an ambitious financial risk by planning a daily broadcast, from six in the morning until midday, lasting two months. Loans, sponsorships, grants and koha enabled a paid staff to produce a parakuihi (breakfast) show plus news, current affairs and a rangatahi (youth) show to a surveyed audience of approximately 20 percent of Wellington Maori and 3 percent of general listeners.

Maori radio had arrived and was challenging the status quo. Strictly speaking, it is not tribal radio, as Nga Kaiwhakapumau, the parent body, is multi-tribal. But an example had now been set for other parts of the country to try their hand. Soon aspects of the urban-based model were being adopted around the tribal areas.

Radio Ngati Porou began to beam out of Ruatoria on the East Coast, with hired help from independent Radio Waikato. Tauranga had a short-term broadcast as did Radio Kahungunu in Hastings and Tautoko Radio in Northland. Radio New Zealand now came back with its plans for a Maori radio network based in Auckland and repeated from the Bay of Plenty, Wellington and Christchurch. The Maori Radio Board was appointed as a subcommittee of the BCNZ, and at a setting-up hui the BCNZ chairman, Hugh Rennie, promised establishment funding of $11 million over a three-year period. However, Maori Affairs were approached instead for $3 million funding, with Radio New Zealand to allocate $1 million from its own sources. As things turned out, Maori Affairs gave about half a million dollars, with RNZ contributing an undisclosed amount. All this resulted in a six-week broadcast in 1988 in Auckland.

Government dissatisfaction with the use of resources by the Maori Radio Board caused a shake-up of membership, but by the end of 1988, little on-air progress had been made. Instead, the Government suggested the board become a private trust, which it did. The Labour Government had signalled they were to deregulate broadcasting and all broadcasting had to pay its way.

The new Public Broadcasting Commission, through recent legislation, is required to have regard for Maori language in its funding of social objectives. Radio Aotearoa, and tribal stations such as Te Upoko, have applied for funding alongside state and private concerns. As a result of $1.4 million government funding, Radio Aotearoa recommenced limited broadcasting to Auckland listeners in June 1989.

As Derek Fox comments, 'Because Maori missed out on the good times when money was available to establish broadcasting, they're now told, "We've deregulated the market, go get 'em!" ' State broadcasting had never invested in developing Maori programming or staff with any real commitment, and found it impossible to suddenly change tack. In 1942 Wiremu Parker had found good-will but no committed support. Forty years later RNZ staffer Piripi Walker faced the same frustrations and took his expertise outside state broadcasting to pioneer Maori radio with Te Upoko o te Ika.

The BCNZ had given staff secondments, hired out old broadcasting equipment, made grants, waived nonpayment of hireage fees, and lived with one or two rebels in their midst, but it had been an uneasy association with Maori radio. Walker relates how former Broadcasting Minister Richard Prebble promised that Maori broadcasting funding in future would be 6 percent of the public licence fee per year, as administered by the new Public Broadcasting Commission. That's around $3.3 million per year — the cost of running one Auckland station.

On 18 December 1988, state broadcasting's assets were to be divided between the state-owned enterprises of Radio New Zealand and Television New Zealand. That was also the date when any Waitangi Treaty obligations between the Crown's agent, the BCNZ parent body and the tribes would cease. A High Court injunction was sought by Nga Kaiwhakapumau i te Reo and the Maori Council to prevent the selling off of national assets. Later that day, the Government agreed to stop the transfer. These stalling actions are delaying the inevitable mushrooming of small regional Maori kaupapa stations, where the model will not necessarily fit in with the ZM youth culture, ZB middle-aged, YA business class and Concert Programme highbrow formats.

At the time of writing, the shape of radio licensing in the future remains uncertain. British consultants believe that New Zealand's broadcasting market needs to be opened up to competition and are recommending a range of ways to auction off frequencies to the highest bidder. No mention is made of equity between Maori and Pakeha and the only social needs the consultants see apply to health, safety and emergency services.

> Providers of social services . . . will be expected to participate in the new market system on equal terms with all other prospective spectrum users, with any financial subsidy required being provided out of general taxation.[1]

The new regime expects Maori radio contenders to compete on equal commercial terms with Pakeha concerns backed by big business. It therefore becomes an academic exercise to vet radio in terms of its portrayal and handling of race relations. Initiatives involving training of Maori journalists have sprinkled Maori faces here and there, but overall control remains firmly in Pakeha hands — in all media. Attitudinal changes have taken place in many Maori and Pakeha hearts, but the substance of the media is unchanged.

Some Maori, through pride or frustration and hurt, are choosing to pursue avenues offering opportunity for separate expression. Others will stay in the mainstream and their take, their expressed concerns, will eventually lead to change. Then, finally, radio will carry a bicultural message that connects our hearts, minds and spirits to this land.

Chapter 7

NEW ZEALAND TELEVISION AND THE DOMINANCE OF FOREIGN CONTENT

Geoff Lealand

Television New Zealand is inappropriately named. In the 25 years or more of television in New Zealand, the content has been largely from somewhere else, local material customarily contributing less than one-third of the messages, stories and faces. This reality should govern any discussion of the relationship between the electronic media and race relations in New Zealand. Although this country's racial mixture of Maori, Pacific Islander and Pakeha is unique, many of its images of race relations are imported, created by the media of the Northern Hemisphere. In the deregulated broadcasting climate of the late 1980s, some predicted that the local contribution will be still further reduced.

In many ways, the domination of New Zealand television by imported images has been inevitable. Television drama, comedy, documentaries and news coverage have always been cheaper to purchase in overseas markets than to make locally. The price differential in the costs of making such programmes is not great. Indeed, it has been claimed that the actual cost, in New Zealand dollars, of creating local television drama is considerably less than that incurred in making a North American drama series. But returns from exports have always added value to American and British television programmes. In addition, the cost price of American exports has always been discounted for the purchaser — discounts that are based on the potential viewing audience in each country. Thus New Zealand, with a viewing audience that has yet to reach 3 million, has been charged a minimal amount for its purchases (as we will see later).

The ratings game

Television, the most popular art, has evolved its own genres and styles (as cinema did before it) and these have become internationally recognised. More specifically, American entertainment styles and production values dominate the form and content of television internationally. Even where measures to protect a threatened 'cultural identity' from alleged 'Americanisation' result in favoured treatment for local production, what usually results is cheaper copies of American formula programmes. If 'quality' programming is also a goal, then the result is usually cheaper copies of BBC-style costume dramas.

As a popular culture form, television is governed by formula and does not actively pursue enduring art. There are too many hours to fill and too many demands to meet for excellence to be the prevailing ethos. Television does not, and need not, strive for originality. Its creativity flows from the tension between convention (formula or 'continuing stories') and invention (new twists in the plot, new faces, new jokes, new settings). Television has created its own stories and its own way of telling them, and is increasingly self-referential and autonomous. So we have nearly 30 years of the continuing story of a mythical Northern England street (*Coronation Street*) and a decade-long melodrama about a mythical Texas ranch (*Dallas*).

In New Zealand, there has been little deviation from the norm. Television in New Zealand, at a glance, seems indistinguishable from television in the United Kingdom or the United States. But unlike the United Kingdom, where legislated (ITV) or voluntary (BBC) quotas restrict imported programming to no more than 15 percent of television schedules, and the United States, where an enormous local industry and scheduling practice restrict imported content to 1 to 3 percent, there have been no restrictions on the amount of foreign programming on New Zealand screens. The only formal allusion to local content has been the vaguely worded clause in the Broadcasting Act 1976 that instructed the now-defunct Broadcasting Corporation of New Zealand to 'obtain, produce, commission and broadcast a range of programmes [that] reflect and develop New Zealand's identity and culture' (Section 3.1).

The Broadcasting Commission, committed to 'reflect and develop New Zealand identity and culture by promoting programmes about New Zealand or New Zealand interests . . . to ensure that a range of broadcasts is available to cater for the interests of minorities in the community and of women', has a little more guidance, but no more money, to take up the responsibility previously assigned to the BCNZ. It will have an estimated $55 million to spend, but this will not stretch far, especially when around half is likely to be absorbed by non-commercial radio stations. The new entrant, TV3, will be held to its 40-percent-local-production-within-three-years promise (a significant factor in its success in winning the right to broadcast), but TVNZ has said that it will not match this level, as it would be 'unrealistic in a deregulated environment'.[1]

Opinions vary as to what the deregulated climate in 1990 will mean for local television production. Some believe there will be increased production with the arrival of a third channel and open contestability for the broadcasting fee. Others argue that commercial imperatives (ratings) will swamp other considerations, the need to outflank rivals by maximising audiences resulting in minimal attention being paid to minority interests and less money being available for local production. Buying overseas will remain the most attractive option, both for economy and ease. In 1986, for example, the average cost of one hour of New Zealand-produced drama ranged between $300,000 and $500,000. The high-budget period drama *Adventurer* cost $1.2 million per hour to produce, while at the other end of the scale, the low-budget domestic drama series *Open House* cost a mere $120,662 per hour.

Television in New Zealand has always tended to live beyond its means. But compare the cost of the above two programmes with the average cost to New Zealand of one hour of imported US drama in 1986: $2,600 (Asare, 1986:6). In mid-1988, TV3 complicated matters by beginning negotiations with overseas suppliers, offering higher prices than had customarily been paid by TVNZ. Their activities mean that TVNZ no longer has a monopoly on imports, the cost of imports has increased (so that some series and films may become too expensive for New Zealand screens), and there will probably be even less money available for local production.

In addition to TV3, market analysts are talking of up to 'five more television channels within 10 years'.[2] Even TVNZ seems convinced that foreign satellite signals are likely to reach New Zealand within the next five years. But all such predictions are one-dimensional, based on an optimistic belief in the expansion of the advertising dollar. They also fail to include any investigations of consumers' desire for more television, or their ability to pay for it.

Even if media choices do proliferate, content is not likely to broaden. Multiplicity is not the same as diversity; what it really means is *more of the same*. TV3 will give us more New Zealand programming — a promised 40 percent more — but this increase must be balanced against the addition of many hours of foreign programmes. All recent content analyses of New Zealand schedules confirm that overseas programmes dominate. In Tapio Varis's 1971 *Inventory*, for example, New Zealand was fourth in an international list of television importers, with 75 percent of programming being imported. A survey[3] of television schedules for July–September 1988 showed that a total of 26 percent New Zealand content screened on TV One and 14 percent on Network Two (now Channel 2). In the week ending 2 September, there was only 30 minutes of locally made drama (*Bert and Maisie*) on TV One. Locally produced television plays, drama series and documentaries have always been rare. The New Zealand contribution to schedules has primarily been in 'factual' television, such as news and current affairs, sports and children's shows and service programming.

Ethnic minorities, race relations and overseas television

More than 25 years of colonisation of New Zealand television schedules has meant that our understanding of race relations has often been influenced by overseas sources. This has meant that we have shared the shortcomings of British and American (and, more recently, Australian) television when it comes to the representation of race relations. Black, brown or yellow faces are a rare sight on British television, which has, by selection or omission, perpetuated and given 'common sense' credence to racist myths:

> News is curiously selective. When Haiti liberated itself, four news programmes chose to do in-depth coverage of voodoo in Haiti. . . . Why isn't there nightly news on racial attacks in this country — like the relentless coverage of violence in Northern Ireland?[4]

As black journalist Ronnie Smith points out in the same article, racism in the British media is not the result of an organised policy 'to deliberately reinforce and bolster black stereotypes'. Journalists, television producers and programming executives may not individually be racist, but their *modus operandi* is. Entrenched practices (news selection and news editing) and a certain lack of self-interrogation promotes and perpetuates racial stereotypes, sustaining or transforming ideologies, generating interpretations of social realities which viewers find credible or justifiable.

In other areas of British television, ethnic minorities remain marginal or one-dimensional. Black actors are more likely to play villains than heroes in drama (in *The Sweeney*, for example, villains were often West Indian or residents of ambiguously named African states); or play the genial fool in the occasional sit-com. With its brief to serve minority interests, Channel Four has offered different perspectives, with examples of mainstream multicultural programming that are sensitive to both racism and the need to entertain and inform. Unfortunately, well-scripted and funny series starring West Indian or Asians (such as *No Problem!*, *Tandoori Nights* and *Desmond*) seldom reach New Zealand screens.

Racial minorities fare better on American television, and New Zealand viewers have seen a lengthy list of programmes that feature black Americans as strong central characters (*Miami Vice*, *Hill Street Blues*, *The A-Team*), or series that feature all-black casts (*The Cosby Show*, *A Different World*). But ethnic minorities in the United States have not always enjoyed the success of *The Cosby Show* and its ilk. A survey of the traits of characters in television shows from 1955 to 1986 has revealed that the early shows tended to present a 'monochromatic world', and until the mid-1960s only about one character in 200 was black.[5] In later years interracial law enforcement teams became 'a prime-time cliché', glossing over real racial tensions. From the mid-1970s, there was a revival of the ethnic sit-com and crime shows with ethnic characters in the cast, but this meant villains as well as heroes. Hispanics, in particular, 'were among the nastiest criminals on TV in the 1980s'[6] in shows such as *Miami Vice* and *Hill Street Blues*. Blacks fared better in the 1980s, largely escaping criminal portrayals while enjoying new star-ring roles (Bobby Hill in *Hill Street Blues*) or quietly providing positive role models (Heathcliff Huxtable in *The Cosby Show*), as they have 'gradually progressed from invisibility to integration into TV's fantasy world'.[7]

But to many black Americans, these portrayals remain fantasies. Shows like *The Cosby Show* are criticised as presenting a privileged, white copy world of little relevance to the experience of most blacks. Meanwhile, Hispanics have not fared well; their television characters 'span a narrow spectrum from villain to second bananas [supporting roles] . . . making it hard to resist the conclusion that Hollywood has cracked open the door to black concerns while letting Hispanics serve as window dressing'.[8]

How American television treats racial minorities is of importance to New Zealand. British and Australian programmes do not show the same attention to race relations. Shirley in *Coronation Street* and Carmel in *Eastenders* are the exception, rather than the rule, and we have yet to see an Aborigine in *Neighbours*. Most popular American series are likely to be screened in New Zealand, attracting large audiences in prime-time slots. In 1987, *The Cosby Show* was the most popular drama show for the year, attracting 42 percent of all New Zealand viewers for its 4 July episode.[9] Such fictional views of America can be influential in rein-forcing New Zealanders' preconceptions about American society, for they are read as representations of that society. Even a programme that strives to be 'naturalistic', such as *Hill Street Blues*, does little to dispel the prevailing view that American streets are violence-ridden and rife with racial tension.

American television programmes have nonetheless failed to inculcate American beliefs in New Zealand. Media imperialism has succeeded in an economic sense, disadvantaging local programming in the ways already outlined, but not in a cultural sense. The American television world remains an alien domain for New Zealanders; it is its foreignness, in fact, that is the primary reason for its appeal, especially for the young. It looks and sounds different and tells different stories from any other television. A major component of this exoticism is its racial diversity; the visible presence of diverse ethnic minorities is remarkable, sometimes strange and sometimes threatening. But, as Fiske points out in his *Television Culture*, the portrayal of ethnicity in popular culture such as American television programmes can be a source of identification for minorities elsewhere in a way that transcends official national cultures.

> A national culture, and the sense of national identity which many believe it can produce, which is constructed by the cultural industries or by politicians or cultural lobbyists, may not coincide with the social alliances that are felt to be most productive by subordinate groups within the nation. Thus Aboriginal cultural identity within contemporary Australia may serve itself best by articulating itself not with an Australian nation, but with blacks in other white-dominated, ex-colonial countries.[10]

This may explain the ready adoption by Maori youth of manifestations of black American culture, ranging through breakdancing and street graffiti, to rap and hip-hop music. Such elements of American culture are seen as more appropriate and closer to their own experience than the 'quality' content (that is, British, or its local equivalent) so highly valued by cultural conservatives.

New Zealand television and race relations

Obviously, much about race relations is learned from this exposure to imported images. But how does television in New Zealand perform in providing images of the unique ethnic mix in this country? If imported images provide a distorted, or incomplete, vision of ethnic diversity, how well has locally made television done in redressing this imbalance, or in giving its own version of New Zealand's ethnic diversity?

Generally, not very well. Programmes which deal directly with Maori or Pacific Island issues, speaking in a Maori or Pacific Island tongue, are few and are generally scheduled out of prime viewing times. *Te Karere* is more accessible in its early weekday evening slot, but goes into a lengthy hibernation over the summer. There has been some public discussion about the desirability of subtitling (translating) the content of *Te Karere* to enable non-Maori-speaking viewers to share this programme. The primary role of *Te Karere*, however, is to provide Maori news for Maori speakers — one tiny voice amongst the din of English and American accents. Further programming in Maori may be constrained more by a lack of resources (especially trained Maori-speaking staff) than by institutional hesitation. One of the strongest elements of the residual 'public service' brief of television in New Zealand in the 1990s is a commitment to the continuance and extension of Maori and Pacific Island programming, even though it has been a hard and long battle to achieve present levels. The failure of the Aotearoa Broadcasting System to win the right to a Maori-controlled channel (see chapter 19) is not yet a dim memory.

If television is to play a crucial and leading role in promoting racial harmony and the notion of sharing as set out in the Treaty of Waitangi, there is a need for a firm and unswerving commitment to presenting different languages and different perspectives. But more importantly, if Pakeha are to learn that Maori and Pacific Island concerns also connect with their own lives (that issues of land rights, language preservation and cultural identity are central to the social future of New Zealanders), there is also a need to raise the visibility of ethnic minorities in the *mainstream* of New Zealand television programming. This means a more integrated television than we have now: that is, more Maori, Pacific Island, Indian and Chinese characters in drama and comedy; as participants in game shows, children's programmes and televised sports; and most particularly, more positive images to counter the prevailing negative caricatures of Maori-as-criminal or Pacific Islander-as-overstayer which dominate network news. The popularity of the comedy of Billy T. James and of Olly Ohlson (and his successors) on children's programmes demonstrates that viewers, young and old, welcome a Maori presence on their screens. Also, if Maori and Pacific Islanders are to share in all aspects of television, their absence from advertisements (see chapter 10) must be redressed.

In January 1989, Television New Zealand's Maori programmes department announced its intention to follow this route by producing music programmes featuring Maori artists but designed for mainstream viewer appeal. Department head Ernie Leonard commented: 'There has been a notion that Maori programming is "narrowcast" and only for Maoris, and I beieve these music programmes blow that notion to hell.'[11] In addition, Maori drama would be regarded as 'potentially commercial television'. To some extent, this may be anticipating TV3's plans to concentrate on 'mainstreaming' its own Maori content.

Increased visibility will also result from increased numbers of Maori and Pacific Islanders working in television, to swell the currently very low numbers both sides of the camera. Television New Zealand has already made commendable moves in this area. It will be more difficult to introduce change in the television product: to 'colour in' the current rather pale representations of New Zealand society on our screens. There is a need for time (the period allowed for submissions to the 1989 Broadcasting Bill was not long enough) to enable television to investigate its practices and to assimilate the educative function of television, for when broadcasters are seen in their practice to be anti-racist, viewers will be encouraged to follow suit.

There is also a need to develop greater understanding of audiences. There is little audience research in New Zealand beyond ratings (quantitative measurement of audience numbers), and these fail to differentiate audiences other than by age, gender and whether they do the household shopping. They do not differentiate viewers by their ethnic background. For example, little is known about the viewing references of Maori and Pacific Islanders and whether or not they constitute a special audience; they are simply treated as part of a largely homogeneous general audience. This gives further weight to calls for greater participation by Maori and Pacific Islanders in mainstream programming and for support in developing their own media.

Television New Zealand executives claim that the audience for programmes such as *Te Karere* tends to be white and affluent, but such a claim is based on flimsy evidence. There is a need for qualitative, culturally sensitive research and educational initiatives which will increase our knowledge about the place of ethnicity in media consumption. There are plenty of good research models to follow, such as Atkin, Greenberg and McDermott's investigation of television and ethnic role socialisation in Michigan and California. And the work of Australian teachers in reassessing media stereotypes of Aborigines should inspire their New Zealand counterparts.

It is time also for a drastic revision of conventional notions of a mass media audience, to acknowledge the impact of technological change in New Zealand and the role of an active audience in determining the content of the media. The spread of remote control devices, multiple-set families and video recorders has enabled viewers to take a more active role in selecting and filtering media content. Perhaps it is now as appropriate to look at the portrayal of ethnic stereotypes on rental video cassettes as on prime-time television.

Nonetheless, prime-time television will remain the major source of mediated images of ethnic and race relations for the 40 percent or more of New Zealanders nightly waiting to be educated and entertained. There can be no arguments against an increased, culturally sensitive Maori and Pacific Island presence on this nightly television menu. And it should be on their terms, observing their traditional ways and perspectives on the world. Yet to some extent, it also has to be on television's terms, observing the strengths and weaknesses of the medium. Although there is a place for serious programmes (considered studio discussions of Maori issues, for example), there is also a place for frivolity and lightheartedness, celebrating both the rich vein of Polynesian popular culture and the rich entertainment potential of television to the benefit of all of us.

Chapter 8

TALKBACK RADIO: AIRING PREJUDICE

Lesley Max

In its infancy in the early 1970s, talkback radio offered every New Zealander with a telephone the miraculous opportunity to communicate his or her thoughts with hundreds of thousands of people. Early hosts, such as Bruce Slane, Brian Brooks and a younger, more moderate Syd Jackson, opened doors to new worlds. The spontaneity, immediacy and participatory nature of the medium presented endless possibilities — not least, it seemed, for reducing racial prejudice.

As talkback ends its second decade, it is possible to examine certain of its structural aspects which have a particular application to matters of race relations. The example of the Jewish community's experience will be used here. Frequent reference will be made to Radio Pacific, but this should not be interpreted as a general condemnation of the station, which has been responsible for many high points in talkback broadcasting. Radio Pacific was established in south Auckland with the aim of celebrating the ethnic diversity of the largest Polynesian city in the world. However, its format failed to attract the targeted audience and the station was compelled to change its programming in order to survive.

Talkback has offered an unprecedented gift to people with a message to impart. It costs nothing, requires no effort beyond picking up the telephone, and can carry a minority message, anonymously and instantly, to thousands. But there's a thin line between healthy public debate and the flogging of prejudices to an audience undreamt of by the pamphleteers.

The medium is not covered adequately in the old Broadcasting Act. Such phrases as 'standards which will be generally acceptable in the community', 'standards of good taste and decency' and 'accurate and impartial gathering and presentation of news, according to recognised standards of objective journalism' are scarcely adequate when applied to a medium which operates 24 hours a day, is accessible to the public on a seven-second delay, and is entirely subject to the whim of the caller, who may be drunk, maudlin or hot with rage. The host has just seven seconds to assess a statement for possible defamatory content. Under such conditions inflammatory statements are of course sometimes broadcast.

The only comparable avenue of public expression is the newspapers' letters to the editor columns, though here there is a cooling-off period while the letter is written and posted; it will usually pass through the hands of at least two editors as it is considered for publication; and a name and address are required, as few reputable newspapers tolerate pseudonyms. Talkback hosts have an opportunity, indeed a ratings-driven requirement unparalleled in other media, to editorialise.

There is no 'border' around the host's opinion, as there is around the newspaper editorial, to separate it from 'objective' reporting.

An ephemeral medium, talkback radio currently carries no requirement that a publicly available record be kept of exactly what has been said, so subsequent investigations are extremely difficult. It is imperative, therefore, that there be publicly available recordings, as easily accessible as back copies of newspapers, so that complaints can be sorted out without undue delay or confrontation. At present, at least at Radio Pacific, the management demands precise details of the offending comments — details which cannot be provided without a tape or transcript. It is therefore necessary to make a formal complaint in order to acquire a tape from which one can decide whether or not to make a complaint!

The immediacy of talkback is especially significant in an area as sensitive as race relations. A feature which lends itself to the perpetuation of racial stereotypes is the pseudo-intimate 'mateship' that can develop on the airwaves with a particular style of congenial, usually male, host. To these hosts, many male callers are 'mate', while women tend to be 'love'. The tone is conversational, the content largely an exchange of secondhand clichés, as comfortable and reassuring as a warm rice pudding. The conversation might go: 'I dunno what's happening to the Maoris, mate. Y'know, years ago, we used to live down Te Kuiti way, and we all used to get along together, we played sport together, no difference, we were all just Kiwis. . . .' This provides the cue for the host to deliver a set-piece confirming the caller's attitudes. Common conversational themes include 'Maori stirrers', and the desirability of forgetting all that 'separateness' business and of just getting on with life and being New Zealanders together. A humorous tone here can often disguise damaging innuendo. These exchanges make useful fillers, especially at times when topics of interest are scarce.

Research for talkback programmes tends to be cursory: it may be that the host merely scans a guest's curriculum vitae two minutes before air time. They will seldom have reference materials available in the studio, so they must rely on there being callers with the knowledge to supply balance for opinions a guest or caller may be advancing. There can be no comparison with the time and research that goes into preparing a feature article for the written media, or for a radio or television current affairs feature, yet the intimacy of the medium allows talkback to penetrate the listener's consciousness in a way that other media seldom can.

The public is ill-served when persuasive studio guests with a message to convey encounter hosts who are inadequately prepared. Such was the case with historian David Irving's rehabilitation of Hitler, and with Black Muslim Abdul Akbar Muhammed's representation of his friend Idi Amin as the innocent victim of Western prejudice. The two hosts on the latter occasion, lacking facts which could have been gleaned in two minutes from the *Encyclopaedia Britannica*, fell back on protestations of the 'But I seem to remember' kind. If talkback is to venture beyond the therapeutic chitchat, the sports talk and the horoscopes, all of which it does so well, into serious and sensitive issues, it requires hosts with the capacity to research; it requires support staff to assist them; and it requires scheduling to allow for adequate preparation.

Perhaps the major structural feature of talkback which militates against the sensitive handling of racial matters is ratings. A host who cannot stimulate his or her listeners, who can't provoke or challenge, is likely to rate poorly. The advertising department must consequently lower its charges for that session. Fear and indignation are the most potent motivators for callers. Violent crime, gangs, immigration and the future of lands or fisheries are all current spurs to fear and indignation. A host faced with an empty call 'board' must generate excitement somehow. Topics that rank caller and host against 'them' — whoever 'they' might be on any occasion — are potent tools to make the 'board' light up like a Christmas tree.

The 'board' often indicates the truth of the adage that 'Jews are news', and thus good business for profit-driven talkback with ratings to maintain and endless hours to fill. Over the years, Jewish people have experienced considerable pain and distress as a result of talkback. Those with experience of Europe in the 1930s have talked of the radio as the purveyor of anti-Semitism to the masses. Even now they feel impotent, perhaps because of age, accented English and tormenting memories, to counter the lies they hear repeated.

It was talkback that popularised in New Zealand the concept of 'the Conspiracy', the fantasy which had previously been confined to the pamphlets and meetings of the Extreme Right, the very same fantasy that inspired the Nazi genocide. Jewish listeners have been astounded and offended to find ludicrous allegations being discussed by apparently rational people. Conspiracy-theory exponents, such as the League of Rights' Eric Butler and Jeremy Lee, have been studio guests. Even on *Lilies and Other Things*, Sir Robert Muldoon's down-to-earth session for the ordinary bloke, one may hear a caller giving a lengthy plug for the lurid Jewish-conspiracy book *Warning* recommended by the Sunday Club. Recently, callers to Radio Pacific have been praising a new book, *Save Our Democracy: The New Zealand Story*, as crudely and ignorantly anti-Semitic as any book ever published here.

Pathological hostility infected calls to studio guest Dr Edith Eger, an Auschwitz survivor. On another occasion a discussion labelled 'Torah versus Koran' seemed calculated to promote religious tensions in New Zealand. The host, a former disc jockey who handles the Sunday request session charmingly, was entirely out of his depth. Bitter antagonism frequently characterises discussion of the Arab/Israel conflict, as the following excerpt illustrates. From the introduction listeners might have assumed they were about to hear a rational discussion.

Felix Donnelly:
Welcome to our show. . . . Our guest at the moment is Dr Ron McIntyre, who is . . . speaking tomorrow at the Palestine Human Rights Campaign meeting . . . as he looks at the problems of the Middle East and in particular at Lebanon.
Harry, a caller from Christchurch:
My uncle, who was a learned person, said that the Zionist movement were the most unscrupulous people in the world and if they couldn't rule the world money-wise in the way of capitalism they would do it in the mind of a dirty little Jew called Lenin who was a Bolshevik. . . . They won't be satisfied until they rule the world. . . . The Zionist movement is the most powerful movement in the world. . . . They control all the arms in America, in Western Europe etc. They've caused all the wars throughout the world. . . .

In the '30s, why did Hitler declare war on the Jews more or less and have them put to death and what have you?. . . The Jews were the only ones who had businesses and money. . . . His people were getting carried away, babies in wooden boxes . . . the Jews were running the country. . . . The observation I can make is that it was unfortunate that all the Jews weren't in Germany at that time and he may have been able to put down more.

The only protest the listening public heard from the doctorate-holding university lecturer guest on 'information radio' was to Harry's regret that Hitler had not been able 'to put down more'. Talkback had permitted Harry to assert, without contradiction, that Jews/Zionists are dirty, treacherous, unscrupulous conspirators, unimaginably powerful, rapacious, profiteering, the controllers of all arms and the instigators of all wars. Such exchanges confirm talkback as the defamer's dream.

The Broadcasting Act 1976 requires broadcasters to 'have regard for the privacy of the individual', but says nothing about the privacy of the group. Thus, a group of people, by virtue of birth, find themselves forever drawn into an argument which they did not choose, living with a tape recorder at the ready, tutored by the Holocaust to fight the poisoning of public opinion. And to fight means discussing publicly matters of heart and 'gut' and soul, of family and identity, of faith and tradition. Should a Jew have to expose this taonga, or treasure, in the talkback marketplace? Should it not be possible to discuss the legitimate differences of approach to the Middle East questions without racist innuendo and invective? Holocaust survivors find it virtually impossible to tell their *own children* what anti-Semitism became in Auschwitz. How can they tell the Harrys?

Conclusion

Despite initial idealism and much positive achievement, and despite the fact that most hosts are well meaning, talkback radio has proved a gift to those infected with the most ineradicable racism in the world's history. There is a notion abroad that it is somehow good and healthy merely to ventilate issues, and that, in so doing, the wheat will be sorted from the chaff. Listeners, it is assumed, know the truth when they hear it, even in matters remote from their own experience or knowledge. This notion provides a rationale for the abrogation of broadcasters' responsibility to research, to question and to balance.

The technology of talkback preceded a coherent philosophy to guide it, as is also the case with access radio. Melbourne's ethnic access station, 3CR, has demonstrated the difficulty of reconciling passionate political and national opinion with responsible, non-defamatory broadcasting. In multi-ethnic communities, access radio can, ironically, exacerbate the very tensions it was intended to relieve, as the conflicts of the Old World are rehearsed in the New.

If both 'broadcast' talkback and 'narrowcast' access radio are to live up to their potential to educate, entertain, inform, involve, and to reduce racial barriers between people, close attention should be paid to developing a coherent philosophy and an operating structure under which the rights, beliefs and sensitivities of all social groups are protected.

Chapter 9
ACCESS RADIO: MEETING MINORITY GROUP INTERESTS
Peter Tohill

The history of New Zealand broadcasting is strewn with stops and starts and conflicting debate over efforts to meet the needs of minority groups. The Broadcasting Act 1964 required the then Radio New Zealand 'to ensure that programmes reflect and develop New Zealand's identity and culture'. Despite this statutory obligation, the public broadcasting system has remained primarily monocultural in both philosophy and content. There have been changes in recent times, particularly in regard to Maori radio. Unfortunately, the pace and degree of change has not been sufficient to have had a noticeable effect on the services provided to minority groups. The needs and aspirations of these groups have, however, been met to some degree by access radio.

What is access radio?

Access radio involves community-based radio stations in which minority groups have an opportunity to prepare, present and broadcast independent radio programmes. It provides these groups, and individuals, with an opportunity that they would not otherwise have because they are under-represented in the mainstream media. Neither public nor private broadcasting systems normally allow minority groups the opportunity to present their language, culture, music and views to their own communities. Access radio aims to fill this need. It also aims to remove the so-called electronic mystery of radio and to make it accessible to people in the community. By being part of access radio, minority groups are able to express themselves to their own people, in their own language. At the same time, access radio provides the wider community, at least potentially, with an insight into the needs and aspirations of the minority groups in our society.

Access radio and Radio New Zealand

Radio New Zealand established access radio in Wellington in April 1981. It began as a pilot scheme with the ultimate goal of setting up access stations in other areas. This long-term goal was never achieved. Access Radio Wellington continued to be the only station fully funded (more than $250,000 in 1989) and supported by Radio New Zealand. User groups in Wellington received access services free of charge, and technical and professional staff support from Radio New Zealand.

Stations in Christchurch, Masterton and Auckland have received either limited or nil support from Radio New Zealand. Since 1987 Radio New Zealand has officially ceased to accept responsibility for new access stations.

This haphazard and inconsistent approach has severely restricted the growth of access radio on a national basis. Clearly the public broadcasting system has not met its statutory obligation to 'reflect and develop New Zealand's identity and culture'. The Broadcasting Act 1989 and the new system of funding contained in it should help to correct the balance. However, regardless of the possible benefits of the new policy and system, the fact remains that Radio New Zealand's past record with regard to minority group broadcasting is abysmal.

Access radio: the model

There has been no single model for access radio, because governments over many years have lacked a consistent policy with regard to minority group radio broadcasting. Party manifestos have been strong on rhetoric but very weak when the broadcasting needs of minority groups needed to be addressed. And Radio New Zealand has lacked a strong commitment and clear policy to meet its statutory obligations.

As a result of this inconsistent and confused approach to development access radio has evolved piecemeal, in a variety of ways in different places. Different methods of operation are not wrong in themselves but have inhibited the national growth of access radio. Wellington Access broadcasts through 2YB for 30 hours each week. It occupies studios and offices in Broadcasting House and receives full funding from Radio New Zealand. Broadcasters do not pay for air time. Plains FM Christchurch are in quite a different position. The station is closely allied to Christchurch Polytechnic, but in order to function it relies heavily on commercial sponsorship, advertising and loan finance. Minority group involvement in Christchurch is still developing. It currently broadcasts for approximately 30 hours per week, and Christchurch broadcasters pay an average of $60 for an hour-long programme.

Access radio in Masterton and Auckland is different again. The former is located in a large rural community and broadcasts from studios at Wairarapa College. It has air time on Radio New Zealand station 2YD for three hours each Sunday night. Access Radio Masterton's problems in finding the necessary operating finance have meant supporters have spent more time fundraising than broadcasting.

Access Radio Auckland has also received very little official Radio New Zealand support. It broadcasts for 20 hours per week using 'downtime' on 1YC AM. Since early 1989 Radio New Zealand has charged for the use of this air time. Access radio broadcasts in Auckland are financed primarily by broadcasters paying a fee of $80 per hour of air time. In more than two years of broadcasting, more than $80,000 has been spent to ensure minority groups in Auckland have an opportunity to broadcast.

Access Radio Auckland — a possible model for ethnic minority groups

The difficult circumstances faced by Access Radio Auckland have, over time, proven to be a source of strength. It has had to establish itself and to operate without a major benefactor, such as Radio New Zealand or a polytechnic. From the beginning its strength has come from the community at large; this has become a key element in both its success and its survival.

Since the first broadcast in April 1987, 157 community groups have used access radio in Auckland. Twenty-three of these groups have come from the wide range of ethnic minority groups that contribute to the social and cultural crucible of Auckland. These multilingual and multi-ethnic groups present up to 30 percent of the programmes broadcast — a high percentage in proportion to the total number of groups broadcasting. The broadcast hours presented by Pacific Island groups exceed by a substantial margin the total number of hours broadcast by Radio New Zealand Pacific Island broadcasts. All groups present programmes in their own language. This is not only a viable means of communication within their communities, but also contributes to the maintenance of their languages and the strengthening of the identity of each group.

Access Radio Auckland has existed on the barest of financial and other resources, yet has achieved a good non-professional standard of community broadcasting. The key to its success has been the sound community base and the commitment of the people involved. There is the stationery clerk, for instance, who provides technical assistance with programme production, the office manager who produces and presents programmes in both English and her own language, the factory inspector and the security guard who prepare programmes and operate studio equipment for their minority groups. Then there is the group of young people from another minority group who, after starting with no broadcasting experience at all, now produce and present a programme every week. To all these people, the mystery of radio broadcasting has been removed. They, and others like them, have learned radio craft and today they can, with new-found confidence and enthusiasm, use radio for the benefit of their own communities. This is the essence of access radio.

The implications: access radio and race relations

Radio still has immense power to create and sustain public perceptions of minority groups. It remains the most mobile and accessible vehicle of the electronic media. Reaching its audience 24 hours a day, radio makes contact with people in the workplace, the kitchen, the garden, the car, the beach, and a host of other places. It therefore has a major role in influencing the change from a largely monocultural society to one that accepts and understands the value of a diversity which represents the many ethnic groups and cultures in our society.

In the past the interests and aspirations of minority groups have been ignored by public and private broadcasting systems. The confused and half-hearted approach to the establishment and maintenance of a fully effective national access radio system reflects this situation. The establishment of the Broadcasting Commission and its objectives recognise this failing. The commission has responsibilities which include the provision of funds to

- reflect and develop New Zealand identity and culture by promoting programmes about New Zealand or New Zealand interests, and to
- ensure that a range of broadcasts is available to cater for the interests of minorities in the country.

Conclusion

Access radio, when provided with the resources it needs, can be a forum and conduit for social contact and interchange for the diverse groups which make up our society. The part played by this medium must be officially recognised, and its resources increased, so that it can make a full contribution to the creation of tolerance, understanding and a willingness to accept people's differences. Access radio provides an opportunity for these differences — in language, culture, music, philosophies, and so on — to be accepted as a source of strength rather than weakness in our society.

Those involved have found that access radio is more than just a way of presenting their message to a wide audience. It has also become a channel through which ethnic and other minority groups make direct contact with each other. In normal circumstances, people from such a wide range of cultures would not meet. Through access radio, they do; they work and learn together, and share the frustrations of making a radio station operate on a 'shoe-string'.

Many individuals, both within and outside the minority groups, now admit to having their stereotypes of other people changed through listening to access radio. They have learned that there are cultural values and customs other than their own that are worthy of being accepted. As access radio grows and strengthens, so will its contribution to inter-ethnic understanding and tolerance.

Chapter 10
WHITEWASH: THE ACCEPTABLE IMAGE IN TELEVISION ADVERTISING
Mark Scott

For Mother's Day in 1989, a Golden Kiwi advertisement will feature a Maori mother, breakfasting in bed and being surprised with her family's gift of a lottery ticket. The discovery that non-whites live in families in houses and give each other gifts will be an industry first. Everywhere, the all-white ads we see on television and in print are no accident: the New Zealand advertising industry routinely and expressly excludes Maori and Pacific Island talent — on the grounds of their race alone.

Bob Harvey, of Auckland's MacHarman Ayer: 'In a country that likes to think it's multicultural, there are more dogs shown on commercials than there are Maoris and Polynesians. It is deliberate . . . the view is they have no image appeal — except in association with fast food. There is a whole class of clients who would be horrified if you showed a Maori or a Polynesian in their showroom.'

May Abbott, the director of one casting agency, said blanket refusals on the grounds of race were so much a fact of life that she was unable to accurately isolate any one company. I learned later, from a different source, that Abbott had recently experienced just such a refusal — to even consider viewing alongside the Pakeha offerings a couple of suitable non-whites for the role of laboratory assistant. The production house responsible reacted with hostility. 'There is no problem using ethnics except where you have the managing director of a company turning out to be from the Cook Islands.' What about laboratory assistants? 'How did you find out? Who told you? You have no right to publicly ask questions about selection criteria.' The next day, I got a distressed call from Abbott, who said she'd been threatened with having her business destroyed if she named the company.

Apart from the ethics of confidentiality, Abbott, like everybody else in the industry, was not about to risk her livelihood by confirming names. She was in no doubt about another variety of ethics. 'People should be chosen on their merits and not on the basis of their colour — and, dammit, that is not happening. Is that what New Zealand is supposed to be about?' When Abbott was first asked to provide Maori extras (for a television programme), she advertised at the Labour Department. 'One Maori, very dark skin, was a university graduate who'd also

This article first appeared in the Listener *(12/11/88) and is reproduced here with the kind permission of the* Listener *and the author.*

completed two drama courses. He'd never got on to agency books because, he said, nobody wanted a Maori. He'd done all the correct things and he'd lost faith in himself. There were others like him . . . I thought that was a tragedy.'

There is usually no need for a specific 'non-ethnic' ruling. A producer with another film company: 'If they ask for a dad, it's my experience they mean a European dad — send along a Polynesian and they'd want to know why you were wasting their time. So you don't.' There is no difficulty using non-whites whose race can't easily be placed — a number of those who pass keep their racial identity secret by using European names.

One casting agency, two years ago, tried unsuccessfully to specialise in providing 'ethnics' (the industry term). Margaret Purkis: 'I would suggest there were beautiful Maori kids or that we had a group of very handsome well-spoken Maori or Polynesian men. The production companies would answer that they'd lose their clients.' Purkis was caught in a subtle double bind where, if clients did want obvious Maori, they were Maori who wouldn't upset the 'hori' stereotype — the very stereotype that prevents the wider use of Maori to begin with. 'I didn't want to supply Maori who would be used as caricatures.' Brent Marshall, of Marshall Arts production house: 'In areas where it is really obvious that Maori or Polynesians are large consumers some representation had to happen.' But a fast food ad is typical — two frames of a Maori taking food to his family waiting in a car are overwhelmed by more than 20 frames of a white family, eating at home, a practice apparently foreign to non-whites. Marshall: 'The resistance is still enormous. I will ask a client, "Do you want an ethnic mix?" The answer is most often a simple no. We're doing work now for NEC Computers and the Japanese management insisted we include Maori because to them, it made the ad more like the New Zealand they thought they knew.'

Marco Marinkovitch, of HKM, a leading New Zealand agency, gives an insight into the Japanese mistake: 'Say you were building houses — would you want an ad showing a Maori family moving into one of them? You tend to associate types. Take an image. A Maori, living in Remuera, driving a Mercedes . . . If he drives a Mercedes he's probably a bus-driver — driving a Mercedes, see? You categorise people.' Marinkovitch appeared to be playing devil's advocate. He moved on to the science of quantifying prejudice. 'For market research we have picture sorts — 50 pics of different guys of all kinds, 50 women and 50 dogs. You show groups of people these picture sorts and ask who they associate with a product. For Double-Brown, all the groups picked the Maori tow-truck driver; the same woman and they all went straight to the Dobermann. As an advertiser, we obviously weren't going to have a white guy in a suit to sell Double-Brown. The breweries, on the other hand, would want to move a little upmarket from the tow-truck driver — maybe a more respectable someone driving a big rig worth $300,000, with an Alsatian. If they had a Maori tow-truck driver, a rough-looking tart and a Dobermann, there'd be Double-Brown drinkers who'd say, "Hold on, that's not me." People fantasise. You've got to use everything to optimise the image. You're not going to use a fat slob to sell Stubbie shorts. . . .'

Optimising the image, however, doesn't apply to ethnics. 'There's no way you'd suggest having a Maori or a Polynesian in a suit at a front desk. The sort of image you have is of the ones you see in the streets standing around looking at you sideways . . . rough cars, houses that aren't looked after. We did the Telethon [print] campaign for child abuse and I don't think we were allowed to use Maori for that. . . . I would have. If you were to show Maori as they really are . . . then you'd be really accused of racism.' Marinkovitch is unrepresentative only in that he was prepared to put his name to a deliberately revealing insight into the industry's thinking, without himself claiming a higher purpose. (HKM has a better record than Marinkovitch, in his tongue-in-cheek way, likes to suggest. Two Maori women appear in HKM's current Honda campaign.)

Years on from the pioneering Greggs advertisements, which were acclaimed for showing a reassuring multicultural slice of New Zealand life, there may be a gathering industry awareness that Maori and Pacific Islanders exist. But for what role? Don Ryder, of Saatchi and Saatchi: 'As long as it doesn't jar, I'm happy to have as many as is appropriate. We have used ethnic folk as Lotto dancers, in the Europa ad and with the L & P heatwave ad. It was appropriately and taste-fully an entertainment thing — that's where you expect to see them. They're good at that . . . aren't they? . . . I mean, you might get away with an Indian bank manager — there are lots of Indians popping up all over the place. But that would be very unusual for a Polynesian — but perhaps a teller.'

Ryder agreed that casting a Maori as a technician — say, looking into a micro-scope — would also tend to be inappropriate. My question had a specific purpose. Ryder was unaware that in one Telecom ad done by his agency, there was just such an image. It was probably the first time a product ad had shown an obvious non-white doing anything even remotely intelligent. Telecom's own advertising department did the casting. Gail Teale is the department's assistant manager. 'Actually that guy was an employee. Microscopic testing of fibre-optics was his job. He had a great character face and did the job brilliantly. Both jobs — for the ad, and the real one.' It is clear that had the ad been cast according to the industry's prevailing sense of appropriate reality (not just Ryder's), a Pakeha would have got the brainwork — while a Maori played the guitar at smoko?

This kind of industry thinking helps answer the perennial question: Why don't *they* (non-whites) just get on like the rest of us? One answer is because they are not shown getting on, like the rest of us. By exclusion or negative stereotyping, the advertising industry tells non-white kids not to bother with dreams of success. At the same time, it tells the Pakeha that Maori and Pacific Islanders are not capable people. For the kids who struggle above the second-rate image, the crunch comes at job time. Who instinctively gets chosen for the brainwork? Where does the instinct come from?

What is appropriate? What jars? A recent Golden Kiwi advertisement purports to represent New Zealand, but not a single non-white face appears. As a camera swept the full length and breadth of Godzone, showing dozens of people, the soundtrack tells us Kiwis are Kiwis for Kiwis just like you and me. It is a country inhabited exclusively by Pakeha. DDB Needham has the Golden Kiwi account. Managing director Dave Birrell agreed his agency 'should properly represent the people who live in that country'. He said non-whites will be appearing in later Golden Kiwi ads, including the one for Mother's Day, which will feature a Maori family exclusively. It follows the lead taken last year by an Air New Zealand commercial which showed a Maori family catching a plane.

Curiously, it is the imported American experience (*The Cosby Show* in particular) which has made the image of a non-white family doing ordinary Kiwi things seem plausible. In the US, while token blacks initially stood out like sore thumbs, black quotas have achieved their purpose. That Sledge Hammer's boss is black and competent is entirely unremarkable. A similarly positive portrayal of blacks in advertisements is designed to demonstrate enlightened corporate responsibility. It is no big deal that Crest toothpaste portrays a black woman barrister. Here, non-whites have yet to make laboratory assistant. To cross the barrier of tokenism, it is necessary first to reach it. If non-whites stand out, it is because so few have been allowed to appear. (However, the American example has encouraged the frequent use of visiting American blacks — for the international flavour.)

Agencies are starting to get the women part of the equation right. Although 'bimbo' women, whose lives revolve around plotting the destruction of flies, still dominate the screen, some are now allowed to leave the kitchen and to have a worthwhile existence. Not so non-whites — they are denied existence itself. A review of 50 New Zealand product advertisements, featuring hundreds of actors, turned up only four non-whites. But after 10.30 p.m. there emerges a distinctly different New Zealand which is no longer so obviously all-white. That is when the community ads come on at the cheaper rates. Ads for children on afternoon television — while indulging in a disturbing frenzy of hard-sell — did not show a single non-white face in the two sessions I watched.

One of the industry's defences is the lack of easily available trained ethnic talent. May Abbott: 'They have no problem finding ethnic acting talent for *Crime Watch*.' Bob Harvey: 'Lack of talent is a cheap lie. Look at the movies — *Ngati* and so on.' Breakdancing was one area where ethnics were falling over themselves to have their talent recognised. That the skill was itself inspired by a five-minute spot on *That's Incredible* demonstrates the power of positive role models. The dancers got minor recognition in a Honda City ad — the thread was big-city America. But when it came to advertising flowing soap, a breakdancing Pakeha kid got the role. His conspicuous lack of talent was no obstacle.

There has been an improvement. For some reason, hardware retailers are leading the field. Benchmark and Levenes have both used non-whites naturally and prominently. Mitre 10 has a Samoan man and a Pakeha woman doing some interior decorating. Jane Stewart, of Charles Haines, handles the Mitre 10 account. 'We were looking for an upmarket, zappy male. That guy fitted the role. He was the guy that impressed.' The model, Jay Laga'aia, was supplied by May Abbott. She was not asked for a Polynesian, but nor was a Polynesian excluded. Stewart: 'The people [who exclude non-whites] are doing the country an injustice. With all the Maori things going on, unless we prove that we are prepared to be fair, then they've got a point haven't they? I'm not saying I agree with what the Maori are doing, but we can't have it both ways. Ninety percent of your clients will say we don't want to use them. I'd like to think they're prejudiced without being aware of it. Bias is something that's bred into you. Unless children have parents who can correct the bias, then ads are the image of this country they get.' (Stewart is no idealogue. Her agency also features Billy T. James in another Mitre 10 ad, where James can't get his lips around the word ingenious. Coon incompetence stopped being funny in the United States a decade ago.)

Margaret Purkis: 'Exclusion doesn't so much show racism as [it] shows a lack of experience in the wider sense of exactly how Maori and Polynesians really live. The fried-chicken, beer-gutted image actually injures Maori and Polynesian health. It lowers self-esteem. It says healthy food or a healthy body is not for them. . . . It is very difficult to make the connection between a Pakeha doing something worthwhile and a Polynesian or Maori doing something worthwhile. Children feel it the most.' Purkis explains her approach. 'I'd talk about it on a market basis (15 percent of the market is non-white). Maoris buy yoghurt and they'd buy more of it if it wasn't presented as a purely Pakeha product. I'd ask: "Are your clients aware that you're reducing their marketing options? Have you put together a believable picture of this country? Do you think your client would like to be seen working towards the kind of harmonious New Zealand we'd all like to live in?" '

Purkis wants to know what problem the industry and its clients have with idealising New Zealand. 'The industry is saying that people have racist attitudes and they're not going to try to change those attitudes. That amounts to endorsing prejudice. What a great corporate image! And they're partly responsible for the prejudice to begin with! One agency once told me that given the resources and the brief to market good race relations, they could turn around the fear and the prejudice virtually overnight. That shows the power they know they hold.'

The advertising industry and its clients do not have to endorse prejudice. Kentucky Fried Chicken — with their long-running Herbs reggae advertisement for burgers — was initially confronted with a flurry of 30-odd letters demanding the ad be withdrawn because it was too ethnic/nigger: in the context, the words are interchangeable. KFC head office also wanted an explanation. Were Herbs a band of stature, or had the name been dreamed up as an unauthorised reference to the secret recipe's seasoning? Eventually, positive mail overwhelmed the negative. Within a month, the racially vexed had stopped writing. KFC burger sales doubled. Twenty percent of the increase came from Maori and Pacific Island customers; about 80 percent came from ordinary Pakeha for whom the colour of someone on an advertisement is a non-issue.

The KFC experience shows that the industry, by choosing to reflect fringe prejudice, is not only presenting an inaccurate visual image of this country, but is also exaggerating the negative. Bob Harvey: 'You don't say "Oh shit, we'd better put a Maori in there". You do it without thinking because that's what this country is all about. . . . If you want to pretend only Pakehas live in this country, then you should fuck off to Brisbane. New Zealand is not for you. The most constant cultural image of New Zealand we get on television is from ads. It doesn't matter what you're watching . . . right through *Dallas* there are these little grabs, images of us. That it is an all-white image is bloody unforgivable — is that what we want to tell our young?'

The positive potential of advertisements cannot be overestimated. Several years ago, I saw a small Maori/Niuean child respond to a community let's-all-be-good-

Kiwis type ad. At the first sound of the jingle, the boy rushed to the set, pointing to the screen. Presently, in one small corner, there appeared a shot of a Polynesian father and his son going fishing. It was over in a flash. 'That's me. That's me and my dad! My dad!' He was light on his feet with the novelty: *I exist*. The father disguised a smile.

Chapter 11

DEAR READER, DEAR EDITOR: AN ANALYSIS OF EDITORIALS AND LETTERS TO THE EDITOR

Andrew D. Trlin

A newspaper exercises considerable discretionary power in its selection and presentation of news and information. In doing so, it reflects the values of its staff and their perceived mission. An interesting dimension of this discretionary power, and one which highlights the values of those concerned, is the forum provided by editorials and letters to the editor. The former explicitly represent a newspaper's opinion, the editorial writer often taking a stand on a particular issue. By contrast, it could be argued that letters to the editor represent the voice of the public. But do they? They are certainly contributions from outside the newspaper. But even here the publication process for letters reflects editorial values. Which letters are published, and which are not, whether a letter is altered in any way, the heading given to a letter and its prominence in the letters column — all reflect editorial decisions and, over time, an editorial line.

Clearly newspapers have the opportunity to shape and lead public opinion; to enlighten on the one hand and to perpetuate prejudices on the other. My argument is that with Maori–Pakeha relations at a turning point, New Zealand needs enlightened press leadership to counter or at least mitigate a widespread, sometimes virulent, anti-Maori backlash. I have selected as a model, and as a yardstick against which others might be judged, a notably liberal daily newspaper, and examined, for the period 1 July to 30 November 1988, its editorials (10) and the letters (182) on aspects of Maori–Pakeha relations. The newspaper is Wellington's *Dominion* (daily circulation about 76 900 copies in 1988) and the examination was guided by the following questions: What were the main events, issues or topics addressed? What was the predominant position taken towards the Maori and did this vary depending on the topic addressed? Finally, for the letters, was there evidence of a bias in terms of the prominence given to those that were positive (sympathetic) on particular topics?

Dear reader

The most important and frequently addressed subjects in the editorials were the Treaty of Waitangi and Maori fishing claims made under its provisions — hot topics throughout 1988. What was the editorial position? Commenting on the proposed Bill of Rights, the editorial writer approved withdrawal of the Treaty from what had become a 'watered down . . . pretty toothless . . . constitutional watchdog', agreeing that 'it was too important to be treated just as an ordinary statute' (10/10/88). In the context of the editorial, the Treaty was granted the status of supreme law, which it should retain — invulnerable to political whim and a lodestone for compatible legislation. As for Maori fishing claims and grievances, the editorial position was explicit. It was acknowledged that the Treaty guaranteed to the tribes 'the full, exclusive and undisputed possession' of their fisheries (27/9/88) and it was asserted that these 'inalienable rights' (4/10/88) had been 'abused by the dominant Pakeha culture' (12/7/88).

A wrong had to be redressed. The Maori Fisheries Bill, introduced in September, offered Maori the chance to gain 50 percent of the fishery at a rate of 2.5 percent per annum over a 20-year period, but in return they were to surrender (for this period) their right to take fishing claims to both the court and the Waitangi Tribunal. In the editorial writer's eyes, there were hooks aplenty in this proposal. A 50 percent share was uncomfortable alongside the Treaty pledge of 'full, exclusive and undisputed possession', while loss of access to the court smacked of apartheid and could breach article three of the Treaty which bestowed 'all the rights and privileges of British subjects' (27/9/88). Although big changes were required, the settlement was nevertheless supported in principle.

Any lingering doubts on the editorial stance of the *Dominion* would have evaporated in the heat of the assault on the National Party. Responding to the Maori Fisheries Bill, Mr Bolger described it as an unacceptable allocation of resources on the basis of race, and promised that an agreement on these terms would be repealed by National. 'A typical piece of silliness,' responded the editorial writer, from a party 'unable to produce coherent alternative policies' and which often 'preys on interracial fears' (4/10/88). Three months earlier, an editorial had similarly dismissed fishing industry objections to Maori claims and a campaign for a referendum on the Treaty (led by Bob Martin, president of the Federation of Commercial Fishermen) was described as 'silly and alarmist', and an example of 'commercial self-interest dressed up as civic concern' (12/7/88).

A second but related editorial theme concerned the nature and consequences of Maori subordination and disadvantage. Introduced along with the assertion that fishing rights were 'abused by the dominant Pakeha culture' (12/7/88), the message was developed in a harsh critique of the operation of section 9A of the Race Relations Act. The 'urgent issues of our time,' the editorial said, were those of Maori disadvantage 'in terms of employment, housing, education and health,' not the 'trivial complaints of offended . . . Pakehas' under section 9A that consumed the energies of the Race Relations Office (7/9/88). These disadvantages were among the causes underlying the problem of anti-social gangs, such as the Mongrel Mob and Black Power. The long-term answer to the gang problem lay in 'improved home and family conditions, education, employment and concerted community involvement' (27/10/88).

Subordination and disadvantage is not just economic; it also encompasses cultural issues. Tackling language policy, the editorial writer berated the monolingualism of New Zealanders, as illustrated by the RSA's objection to the official use of 'Aotearoa' rather than 'New Zealand'; previous policies that had marginalised Maori language use; and the loss 'in monocultural primary schools' of a mastery of Maori gained by thousands of youngsters in kohanga reo (15/9/88). The problem was certainly not limited to that of language and educational institutions. Psychiatric care remained 'largely monocultural', so much so that, according to the Mason report, 'even at Carrington Hospital's Whare Paia unit, there was little evidence of a Maori perspective . . . [in] the treatment programme' (11/10/88). The editorial writer's support for biculturalism, however, was not undiscerning. An argument that it was 'culturally insensitive to Maori and Polynesian values' to place the child's interests first in new legislation on child abuse was dismissed as 'fatuous'. Cultural considerations were, however, acknowledged to be crucial in dealing with *specific* abuse cases (10/11/88).

Two general conclusions may be drawn from the above. First, the editorial offers an opportunity to express an opinion, explicitly and with authority, on a topic of public importance. Secondly, in line with its liberal stance, the *Dominion* was unequivocal in its advocacy of Maori interests and opposition to any form of racial inequality. For example, the Maori Fisheries Bill was defensible, despite its shortcomings, 'if Maoris really did end up with a half share in 20 years' time' (27/9/88). The *Dominion*, however, sought not just to lead like-minded readers, but to appeal to some of its more conservative audience. Therefore, while a national policy for Maori language promotion was supported as an important expression of cultural equality, it was also deemed to have other benefits: 'confidence in the mother tongue leads to great success in education . . . that means less crime and social trouble' (15/9/88). It would appear that the editorial writer was trying to make a liberal stance on language policy more palatable for a conservative audience concerned with the 'law and order' issue.

Dear editor

A simple method of content analysis was employed to examine the messages presented by letters to the editor. Editorial policy for both the *Dominion* and the *Dominion Sunday Times* is to reserve the right to abridge or decline any letter without explanation. Accordingly, the information recorded relates to two messages: one from the writer communicating a position or attitude on a particular subject, once the message has been vetted by the editor; and one from the editor concerning the value and importance of a letter, as indicated by the space and prominence given in its presentation.

The results revealed that the 182 letters examined were contributed by 150 individuals, of whom 15 wrote two or more letters each (accounting for 47 letters). Regulars, often identified with particular camps or causes, are a well-known feature of letters columns. Here, three of the four most prolific writers (four to six letters each) adopted a distinctly negative stance while the fourth was usually positive or sympathetic to the Maori. In passing it should be noted that editorial policy is to publish letters over genuine names only and not to accept pseudonyms.

Three key features were discerned in the letters. First, as one would expect, they reflected public issues and discussions of the time. In terms of the topics addressed, they included: fishing and land rights (36); the Treaty of Waitangi and the Waitangi Tribunal (18); differences in the needs and provision of services for Maori as compared with Pakeha (12); 'Aotearoa' versus 'New Zealand' (10); and a large general category (106) which encompassed letters addressing one or more topics, such as the origin and meaning of the word 'Pakeha', Maori gangs, aspects of Maori history, racism and the operation of the Race Relations Act, and so on. These letters, of course, were scattered among and competed for attention with many others on matters such as the purchase of frigates, the state of the economy, environmental deterioration and the abortion issue.

A second feature was that just over half of the letters were unsympathetic or hostile to Maori concerns while less than one-third were pro-Maori, and very few adopted a neutral position. The strength of the anti-Maori camp varied from one topic area to another; for example, exactly half of the letters dealing with the official use of 'Aotearoa' were negative as compared with two-thirds on the subject of Maori fishing and/or land rights, while three-quarters opposed provision of services intended to meet the needs of Maori. In the latter category, criticism was often voiced that such service provision produced a Kiwi-style 'apartheid' and was promoted by 'misguided liberals'. Only in the case of letters concerned primarily with the Treaty of Waitangi were the sentiments predominantly positive. The hostile views pervading the letters columns contrasted markedly with the views expressed in editorials.

The third feature discerned in the examination of letters is of particular interest. It was found that letters supporting or consistent with the editorial position were more likely to be prominently placed at or near the head of the letters column than those expressing opinions hostile to Maori concerns. This bias towards sympathetic (pro-Maori) letters, clearly evident for those concerned with the Treaty of Waitangi and the official usage of 'Aotearoa', applied to most though not all subject areas. There can be little if any doubt that the editorial aim was to ensure that the tone or perspective of the letters columns reflected as much as possible the liberal position adopted in the editorials.

Freedom of expression

In essence, two conflicting messages were presented to the general reader. Aside from a satirical piece on kumara (22/10/88), the *Dominion* editorials championed the legitimacy of Maori claims and needs and generally advocated an end to Maori subordination and disadvantage. This stance, it should be noted, was well supported by sympathetic feature articles.[1] Letters to the editor, on the other hand, had a predominantly negative flavour. Support for these views was provided in two substantial advertisements placed by the New Zealand Fishing Industry Association (2/8/88, p.6; 13/8/88, p.6), and in another from the One New Zealand Foundation (6/8/88, p.4) directed against the Treaty of Waitangi.

There is ample evidence of the *Dominion*'s liberal editorial stance on censorship and the Race Relations Act.

> Good race relations will never develop out of forced silence. Extreme and offensive views will not disappear because they are unspoken. At least if they are freely expressed they can be challenged and countered (7/9/88).

Excellent! As the country debates the Treaty of Waitangi as the basis for nationhood and a just society, there is no longer room for fence sitting, for claims to 'objective' reporting and to representing 'genteel middle New Zealand'. On the evidence available, the *Dominion* has confronted and challenged, if not countered, the dogma of monocultural conservatism. Perhaps it is a role well suited to the nation's capital and a captive morning readership of legislators and civil servants. The pity, however, is that elsewhere New Zealanders have not been as well served by other metropolitan newspapers (notably the *New Zealand Herald*) nor by a good many provincial ones (for example, the *Hawke's Bay Herald Tribune*).

Chapter 12

NEW ZEALAND IN FERMENT: VIEWS FROM ABROAD

Stephenie Knight

New Zealand has traditionally been regarded overseas as quaintly British, a friendly place, and home to vast numbers of sheep. The assumption of a harmonious multi-ethnic society was shared by many New Zealanders, but as our perception of ourselves is coming to be re-evaluated, so too is our international image.

Journalists, always alert for signs of political dissension, have found much in New Zealand to write about in the past few years, but have focused particularly on economic policy and race relations, and the interdependence of these two issues. The 1980s will be remembered internationally as a decade of economic crisis, and it is our approach to economic problems, notably Rogernomics, that has attracted most overseas attention, though reports on the Government's unorthodox economic policies have necessarily raised questions about the social cost.

Race relations have come under scrutiny for two reasons of significance internationally. First, it became apparent that the Government would be voted out of office if the 'white backlash' against government initiatives in this area were left unchecked. Labour's anti-nuclear stand, particularly the banning of nuclear ships from New Zealand ports and demands for an end to nuclear testing in the Pacific, has long been an annoyance to major powers such as the United States and France, who have a consequent interest in the Government's defeat.

Secondly, at a time of increasing demands for indigenous peoples' rights New Zealand was seen to be setting important legal precedents. But in order to report issues that journalists readily conceded were complex ones, it was necessary to place them in a historical context.

A 'faceless name'[1] just three years ago, New Zealand has more recently been the focus of considerable overseas media interest, but we have found ourselves under the international spotlight at the very time when the contradictions over our own sense of cultural identity are sharpest. This chapter, taken from a wider research project, examines a sample range of these views from abroad during the past three years. The newspaper and magazine feature articles chosen all include backgrounders on New Zealand's race relations along with analysis of the present social and political climate. The questions guiding the project were: What do they say about us? How is it different from what we say about ourselves? What are some likely reasons for this difference?

The conventions of international news reporting dictate a similarity of content and style through the many articles surveyed. But while they share many themes, the nature of the relationship between New Zealand and each reporting country is plainly reflected in the tone of the items, which ranges from scorn to admiration. The main focus is on recent government activity, particularly the Labour Government's decision, in 1985, to extend the jurisdiction of the Waitangi Tribunal to include hearing grievances dating back to the signing of the Treaty in 1840. The Treaty is explained mostly in terms of the second article in the English version in which Maori tribes are guaranteed control over their lands, villages and all their 'treasures' (taonga). Such a treaty between indigenous people and colonisers is reported as unusual, although the subsequent disregard for the Treaty by the Colonial Government and the methods used to take the land from the tribes are viewed as predictable.

Political initiatives tend to overshadow efforts by Maoridom to bring the injustices of the past 150 years to public attention, and depressing statistics of underachievement are continually favoured over the many positive accomplishments. No mention is made of the impact of events such as the land marches or the occupation of Bastion Point. Also missing is an appreciation of the work of the tribal trusts in presenting their cases to the Tribunal. Rather it is the Government that is always represented as the agent of change.

Parallels in overseas reporting continue in discussion of the 'white backlash'. The dollar value of the land and fisheries recommended for return to the Ngati Whatua and Muriwhenua tribes is reported, though the figures vary enormously according to the source. The economic value of these 'lost' resources is seen as a major contributing factor to Pakeha anger. The reaction of commercial fishermen to the Muriwhenua decision is described more than once as 'apoplectic'.

A common image is of 'normally placid New Zealand' now 'bubbling with social ferment'[2] and of 'the placid surface of New Zealand society . . . being disturbed by the ripples of conflicting cultures'.[3] It is a phenomenon that is apparently *happening to* people, rather than being *prompted by* them, and where blame is levelled, it is the Government that is the target. The Government's motivation for promoting a bicultural society is rarely explained.

Some commentaries published overseas have in fact been written by New Zealand journalists and tailored for overseas consumption. On the whole, these correspondents have produced balanced, sympathetic, historically accurate accounts, but their analysis is often superficial. The perspective is that of an understanding Pakeha, and the Maori viewpoint is expressed in values important to Pakeha: loss of property, lack of educational opportunity and jobs, fear for the future of the young generation, and loss of the language. Some journalists have alluded, albeit cursorily, to the difference in worldview between traditional European-based society and traditional Maori society. Ironically, though, these comparisons have been used to argue the inevitability of serious, possibly violent, conflict between the two main cultures.

This lack of cultural appreciation is commonly regarded by informed observers in New Zealand as the most important factor in the so-called backlash — a misunderstanding of the essence of the grievances and demands for compensation which has developed into a fear of what Pakeha may have to *give up*. This is never explained to overseas readers, just as it is seldom explained to New Zealand readers. An exception worthy of note is a series written by Pamela Bone for the

Melbourne *Age*, which identifies this fear and introduces a little sanity into the backlash debate:

> The nightmares of some Pakeha . . . include a vision of a gang of leather-clad Maori arriving at their front door with an eviction notice signed by the Waitangi Tribunal. Their fears are groundless. . . .[4]

Moral posturing and sensationalism are common, as is a tendency to reflect the reporter's own cultural and political values rather than ours. Especially marked are the contrasting starting points of once-colonised and colonising countries — for example, Indonesia and France.

The sympathy of one once-colonised people towards another is evident in Indonesian commentaries. Although it had its beginnings 'as a colony of British settlers setting [sic] a new life with their sheep',[5] New Zealand has begun 'to move away from its Eurocentric view of the world' and align itself with Asia and the Pacific. Indonesian commentators give an impression of New Zealand which contrasts sharply with more 'Eurocentric' analyses. For them, the turbulent period of New Zealand's race relations was in its past: 'The overwhelming impression from the first 100 years of contact is one of IGNORANCE, BIGOTRY and NEGLECT. . . .'[6] Only now does New Zealand recognise that the indigenous people, as in Australia, have subsided 'under the flood of white people who finally imposed on them their political power, social arrangements, cultural network and ways of life which eliminated their identities'.[7]

New Zealand is seen as having promoted a resurgence of Maori culture and is credited with saving a nearly 'extinct' language.[8] Where United States and Europe-based journalists speak of New Zealand's Maori resurgence in the context of the upheaval of other white nations grappling with the demands of their indigenous populations, Indonesia sees New Zealand from the point of view of its own indigenous people, and sees the Maori as making remarkable progress towards self-determination. Reports from Indonesia also demonstrate a distinct Pacific perspective; the struggle for minority rights and realigning of power is, in their view, being waged in conditions which compare favourably with those in New Caledonia, Fiji, or even Australia.

French media representatives, whose own governments' colonial record in the Pacific is frequently criticised, aim for the moral high ground in their commentary on New Zealand's race relations. In an article headlined 'Better Red than Black', David Lange is accused of caring little about the Maori — 'an underclass living under colonial oppression'. His motives in meeting people like Oliver Tambo, representatives of FLNKS, and the Soviet Foreign Minister are attributed to the socialist Labour Government's sympathy for 'Soviet-backed marxist terrorist organisations'. Support for the anti-French New Caledonian separatist movement is an attempt, *Le Figaro* believes, to make the world forget Lange himself headed a white-dominated state. Not that France is worried, since 'our other neighbours in the Pacific know, though they will not say so, that the French system has long been a multi-racial one, while the Anglo-Saxon one has not'.[9]

In a more recent article, we find rather more balanced reporting. The Treaty is mentioned, as are the familiar statistics associated with racial disadvantage. Views of (conservative) Maori and business leaders are given, and it is noted that compromises have been made on both sides, though there are allusions to political window-dressing. The journalist's sympathies clearly do not lie with the Government, yet nor are they reserved for the Maori, whose past struggles are dismissed derisively: 'For years, Maori protests were confined to a few eccentric individuals, such as the man who bared his bottom to Queen Elizabeth.'[10]

Japanese journalists have also explained New Zealand's race relations in terms of economics. Traditionally 'more British than Britain', New Zealand has had to cut its ties with that country on Britain's entry into the European Community. The two oil crises of the 1970s hit us hard, but it was the Maori who bore the brunt of the subsequent cutbacks on welfare spending. The rulings of the Waitangi Tribunal, however, are perceived strictly in terms of investment. Bastion Point: 'For Japanese interested in tourism investment, it is a most inviting scenic site.' The Muriwhenua recommendations: 'The New Zealand coast abounds with squid, snapper, etc., and provides a bountiful fishing ground for Japan/New Zealand joint fishing ventures.' Land claims:

> Like Switzerland, New Zealand is bountifully endowed by nature. Sheep and cattle graze on the green pastures while the conifer forests are a source of timber and pulp. It is no wonder that the Pakeha are concerned as to what would happen should these lands and forests be returned to the Maori.[11]

Among overseas observers, the British public are probably best informed about New Zealand's race relations apart from readers of the Melbourne *Age*. The furore over the public auctioning of Maori heads in London raised the issue of the treatment of indigenous people colonised by the British. Many of the feature articles about New Zealand in the British press are well researched and 'balanced': that is, no blame is apportioned to either side and a wide range of views are represented which, usually, express intelligent and reasoned thought. Although the preoccupation with economics and its influence on race relations persists, human rights issues are also raised. New Zealand's leadership role in the Pacific is acknowledged, though with the rider that 'New Zealand's stand on human rights internationally depends for its credibility on peaceful race relations at home'.[12] There is less emphasis on the tensions within New Zealand society (possibly because many of the reports are written by New Zealand journalists).

The United States has produced several articles which draw parallels with legal precedents involving treaties and fishing rights with indigenous peoples. These articles tend to be more superficial than those of British and European origin, but important aspects of the debate do occasionally appear. For instance, an article in the *New York Times* drew attention to the Waitangi Tribunal's pioneering determination in 1983 that the Treaty could not be denied without denying Pakeha the right to be in New Zealand.[13] This is a point that is rarely discussed even by New Zealand's own media.

Australia's reporting of New Zealand's race relations is probably the most interesting because it is the most contradictory: it includes the best and the worst. Among the best is Pamela Bone's series on New Zealand's race relations for the *Age*, of Melbourne. She faces some pretty ugly opposition, though — for instance in the Australian edition of *Penthouse* magazine and, to a lesser extent, in the *Bulletin*, both of which claim New Zealand is on the verge of a racial civil war. The 'phenomenon' of gangs, only briefly and occasionally remarked upon in other countries, is grossly sensationalised across the Tasman. An issue of the *Bulletin* which focused on New Zealand race relations (and for which the writers acknowledge the help of 'sister publications' *Metro* and *North and South*, among others) includes an article headed 'After reform, the backlash', which claims: 'Frustration and failure to make it in a Pakeha (white) economy has given rise to the gang phenomenon and naked violence. There have been robberies, rapes and terrorisation throughout the country.'[14] In the same issue, beneath the headline 'New Zealand: A winter of some discontent', readers are informed that 'race relations in New Zealand are marked by fear and aggression, by crime and violence.' Accompanying the feature are two crudely racist cartoons that would have prompted official complaints had they appeared in this country.

Penthouse goes even further:

> There is fear and loathing on New Zealand streets. This is one of the most dangerous societies in the Western world. . . . The incidence of reported rape is the second highest in the West. Seventy percent of all violent crime is committed by Maoris.'[15]

Allusions to 'pack rape', fortified gang bases, weapons hordes, and a race relations 'time bomb' are scattered through the two-part story, which lingers on the details of the Ambury Park rape and the Otara machete killing. Gang members, whose numbers are said to approach five figures, follow politicised and charismatic leaders, form alliances with each other to increase their strength, and build their own separate economic bases. And Maori leaders are 'embracing the bros like long lost sons'.

Suggestions of armed insurrection by Maori are linked to the observation that the armed forces 'are 75 percent Maori'.[16] This fantastic argument does not stand as an isolated case. According to the *Sydney Morning Herald*, 'with the Maori making up 75 percent of New Zealand's armed forces, these activists are not anticipating any serious opposition from the Army'.[17]

Not only do Pakeha live with the threat of a military coup fomented by the 'feared Maori gangs', but there is the spectre of land claims which 'could eventually involve no less than 70 percent — maybe even 85 percent — of the entire country'.[18] This follows the loss of the Muriwhenua fishing grounds — 'We're talking about a billion-dollar industry here'.[19] The predicted transfer of assets prompts the *Bulletin* to ask the question, 'How will they act as landlords?'[20]

With the exception of the *Age*, most Australian journalists are in no doubt about where responsibility for New Zealand's new reign of 'terrorisation' lies: 'For many white New Zealanders, the [Labour] Government is seen to be pandering to the Maoris. And, worst of all, it is seen not to care.'[21] 'The Government is severely embarrassed by its fatal amendments to the legislation. . . .'[22] And by the Waitangi Tribunal, whose 'job is to assess territorial claims in the rather patchy light of the Treaty of Waitangi, a vaguely worded document drawn up by Governor William Hobson's staff in consultation with the Maori chiefs in 1840'.[23]

The reasons for such hostility towards New Zealand relate partly to the complexities of a traditional national rivalry. It is worth noting that one of only two articles published in Australia that were attributed to New Zealand writers is a positive account of the remarkable success and sophistication of nineteenth-century Maori culture, alongside a reasoned analysis of Maori nationalism.[24] There's more than a hint of sibling rivalry in *Penthouse*'s amusement at 'our little brother across the Tasman . . . suffering a profound identity crisis'.[25] But the real antipathy often appears to be political: most of the articles, while purporting to be about race relations, are thinly disguised attacks on the Government, and almost all New Zealand commentary is provided by members of the National Party. The issues are, of course, rarely related to Australia's own social problems. Australia's 'racial underclass' cannot fill the role of the 'enemy within', as is admitted in this little gem from the *Financial Review*: 'Most Australians have no contact with Aborigines and would have little to fear if relations deteriorated.'[26]

Comparison of these various perspectives suggests that journalistic 'objectivity' is applied only in the presentation of statistical information. Most can recite the familiar figures on Maori over-representation in prisons, hospitals and psychiatric institutions. *Most* of the articles agree on *most* of the data. But as soon as they enter the arena of political and social analysis, objectivity disappears under a flood of righteous moralising that more often than not reflects the political relationship between the reporting country and New Zealand. And there is a consistent absence of any reference to the reporting country's own race relations problems.

In general, the overseas coverage shares many of the weaknesses of local reporting, notably the exclusion of important information — the context of the Treaty signing, for example, which granted to European colonists the right to take their place in a country then dominated economically, politically, numerically and militarily by the Maori; and the many successful Maori-initiated development and investment ventures whose goal is economic independence for Maori, regarded by many as the only path to the restoration of mana Maori.

The biggest difference between local and overseas reporting lies in the sensationalism and pessimism of many overseas reports. Characteristically the New Zealand Government is seen as indulging a violent, ungrateful minority. The images of violence and social upheaval scattered through these reports act as warnings to the domestic readership. By exaggerating the tensions between Maori and Pakeha, and between Government and people, the credibility of New Zealand's relatively progressive approach to questions of indigenous rights and power sharing risks being undermined.

Finally, the survey illustrates again how the popular media reflect the values and agendas of the status quo. So long as this persists, New Zealand's attempts to establish a bicultural society will continue to be distorted in order to support the priorities of others.

III

CASE STUDIES

THE EDITORS INVITED a range of people to discuss particular issues with regard to race relations and the media. Some consider very specific instances.

Vern Rice looks at the media's interest in the Maori loans affair and notes that equal attention is not paid to similar (worse?) Pakeha events. Finau Kolo continues with this theme by criticising the reporting of recent violent conflict in Otara. Gordon Campbell shows how the press missed the mark when reporting on 'street kids' in Palmerston North, and Prue Toft discusses the issue of overstaying and the way in which the media quite unfairly encouraged the public to regard Pacific Islanders as the key culprits.

The remaining chapters look at specific developments within the media or at more general coverage as it relates to one group or another. Tipene O'Regan examines the way in which the media have reported the Ngai Tahu claim before the Waitangi Tribunal, while Samson Samasoni reviews relations between Pacific Islanders and the media. He points to the appearance of publications such as *Pasefika* as evidence of major shortcomings in the mainstream media's coverage of matters of importance for Pacific Islanders.

Derek Fox traces the history of television's *Te Karere*, and in a later chapter documents the attempt to establish a Maori television channel by the Aotearoa Broadcasting System Inc. Both highlight the low priority of, and opposition to, Maori television in New Zealand. It is these experiences which encourage such options as tribal radio and other developments which quite specifically address Maori needs.

Chapter 13

TE KARERE: THE STRUGGLE FOR MAORI NEWS

Derek Fox

Te Karere is an institution now — still young, immature and inexperienced, and going through an erratic patch, but at least Maori language news does have a hold on one tiny corner of television time. It would be comforting to think that the programme owes its existence to sensitive and enlightened leadership within Television New Zealand. Yet *Te Karere* got started almost by accident.

There had been pressure. In fact, there had been representations for Maori news back in the 1970s. But the critical decision came in 1982 when Bruce Crossan, the man in charge of news and current affairs, decided there should be some Maori news during Maori Language Week. I was his only Maori journalist and he told me to prepare a two-minute nightly bulletin in Maori during that week.

My brief as reporter/producer/presenter was to pursue the news of the day, write spoken headlines in Maori and present that live on TV Two just before six in the evening, following an English language bulletin. No facilities were provided for the task, which was made more difficult by the fact that it was presented from a one-camera studio with the English language newscaster, John Hayden, reading his material while I sat on the floor awaiting my turn. Once he had finished, I had 10 seconds to get up, slide into the still-warm seat, compose myself and then present.

I accepted the task, but ignored the brief. Instead of news in Maori, I opted for Maori news, and set out to collect material of interest to Maori viewers. It was impossible to do it alone, so I called on two friends, Whai Ngata and Purewa Biddle, for help. I had recruited them into a Maori radio unit some years before and they kindly came to my aid again. Unselfishly and unpaid, they toiled with me for the week.

Each day we begged, borrowed and purloined facilities to gather, edit and transmit film stories of Maori news. We nightly ignored the two-minute length restriction, usually by taking up slack elsewhere in the schedule. Our confidence grew during the week and culminated on the last day, with a first and an as yet unrepeated event for New Zealand television: we presented the English bulletin and the Maori bulletin, *and* introduced the news for the deaf. Later it struck me that even in 1982 the bulletin for the hearing impaired was half an hour long, an allocation the tangata whenua have yet to achieve.

The following week, I was back at my regular job with the current affairs programme *Close-up*. As far as the television executives were concerned, Maori Language Week was over and they'd done their bit. But the issue wouldn't go away. Maori people began to ask why it wasn't possible to have regular Maori news on the public television system of which they were also shareholders. Bruce Crossan and his Director-General, Allan Martin, were unmoved. But people other than Maori began asking questions too. One of them was Dr Ian Shearer, then Minister of Broadcasting. I was filming in Parliament for *Close-up* one day when he asked: 'What plans are there for the introduction of a permanent and regular Maori news programme?' I suggested he should ask Television New Zealand.

Over the next few months, pressure began to build. Support came from an unexpected quarter. The country's newspapers have never felt obliged to print Maori news, but in late 1982 they began running stories asking why Television New Zealand didn't have a Maori news service. While I didn't instigate the stories, I felt the issue was important enough to respond to questions put to me by newspapers. That didn't win me any popularity with my bosses. Twice in late 1982 I was hauled over the coals, firstly by the controller of news and current affairs, Bruce Crossan, and later by the Director-General, Allan Martin. It was to be the first of several clashes with Martin on matters of principle regarding Maori aspirations in the public broadcasting system.

The seed for Maori news had, however, been sown, and despite a lack of nourishment by Television New Zealand, it refused to die. In February 1983, the seed bore fruit with the arrival of *Te Karere*. But like all Maori developments in broadcasting since, it was on a 'minimalist' scale. The new Maori news programme was a niggardly four minutes long, and was broadcast on TV Two, which wasn't received by a large chunk of the country, including huge rural areas of New Zealand principally populated by Maori people.

One area which missed out was the East Cape region of the North Island, with its large Maori-speaking population. After more agitation, it was arranged that they could receive the *Te Karere* signal, but only as a result of an arrangement which saw the TV Two signal thrown onto TV One north of Gisborne by the flick of a switch in Wellington. The cut was crude and was an imposition not made on any other programme or any other audience. Often the programme on TV One hadn't finished before the 'crash-cut'. To make matters worse, it occurred during children's programmes, causing friction between two sections of the audience poorly served by Television New Zealand — children and Maori. Once a whole class from the Tokomaru Bay school wrote to me complaining about my intrusion on their viewing. My reply was the most difficult I have had to compose in 20 years of broadcasting. We were victims as much as they were and we were being pitted against each other by an insensitive Pakeha system.

For all the difficulties though, and there were many, *Te Karere* was on its way. We began with a staff of two — myself and my old colleague Whai Ngata. We shared the roles of reporter, editor, producer and presenter, and it was the beginning of an extremely demanding time in our lives.

We embarked on a punishing schedule. For the first six weeks of the programme we worked every single day, then we had one day off, then worked another three weeks non-stop. We tried to be wherever there was a major Maori event. Of course, we couldn't be everywhere, and had to be selective. We couldn't afford to be sick, so there simply wasn't any sickness in our team. We couldn't attend tangi together, because someone always had to stay behind to mind the show. When one of us did go to mourn a close friend or relative, it threw a phenomenal burden on the other.

Initially we walked a tightrope between being conservative, and certain that we would have a programme that night, and a determination to cover the Maori issue of the day, wherever it was, and whatever it took. It's possible we were meant to fail, but gradually the results of our efforts began paying off. Maori-related news on television until then had been almost always negative — usually involving criticism of a Maori institution, mostly without any opportunity for comment from the Maori perspective. Television news staff will naturally dispute this because from their monocultural perspective, there is only one view — theirs.

I have often wondered why it took so long to get something like *Te Karere* to air. And while I have searched hard to find some other explanation, in the end I keep coming back to prejudice and a lack of respect. There was no respect for Maori language and culture amongst the senior management of Television New Zealand in the early 1980s, and that condition permeated down through the ranks. In an unguarded moment when being pressed on a Maori matter, a senior executive said that he wished Maori people would just go away and set up their own television station. This comment was heard and recorded by one of my staff while covering the event. It was a damning comment from a man who was charged with running a television service which was legally required to 'reflect the culture of New Zealand', and which received the funds fee for that purpose.

Te Karere in 1983 should have been a straightforward news programme, but it had to be more than that. It was the spearhead of Maori language and Maori perspective television in this country. There had been other programmes, such as *Koha*. But *Koha*'s brief was to appeal to the general (read Pakeha) audience. In other words, it was a Pakeha window on Maoridom, not a Maori programme.

While things did get better in the four years I spent with *Te Karere*, niggly impediments continued to plague our development. For example, despite a tradition that where there is a clash for the use of equipment, the first programme going to air is given priority (and *Te Karere* was the first news show to air each night), we were frequently swept aside in the battle for access. Despite our ability to report in two languages — something we often did — our staff were paid much less than their monolingual colleagues. Even the union, which we all belonged to, never delivered any help for its Maori members.

We often came up against petty forms of prejudice, small matters individually, but collectively indicative of our place in the system. For example, in our second year, the entire news area was given a face-lift, with new paint, carpets and blinds — except our room. Instead, we were given the old carpet discarded from another part of the building. As we took on more staff, and required more desks, our needs were met by the purchase of reject Ministry of Works furniture, unlike our colleagues next door. When our room was finally refurbished, it happened so long after the rest of the office that we were accused of getting priority over everyone else!

These things were irritating at the time, but there were, and still are, more damaging examples of lack of respect. For example, for more than 10 years now, there has been an official broadcasting policy of pronouncing Maori words and placenames correctly. Yet despite that policy, and the ready availability of *Te Karere* staff to correct bad pronunciation, the mutilation of Maori goes on with impunity. This is despite the fact that Maori is an official language, and further highlights the arrogance and lack of respect by broadcasting staff for things Maori.

Clashes of will became more frequent as *Te Karere* grew older, and longer. In our third year, we were extended to 10 minutes a night. By then the programme had settled into a well-oiled machine, and we sought more time. We regularly took on specials such as election reports and end-of-year roundups — all in Maori. Almost daily, we suggested stories we thought our Pakeha colleagues should be covering and carrying in their bulletins. We weren't advocates of 'good news', just news about this country and information we thought New Zealanders should have in order to better understand their surroundings. Sometimes it worked; most often it didn't.

In *Te Karere*, we developed multi-skilled people. There was no rigid delineation of jobs. Most *Te Karere* staff, as well as being reporters, were developed as presenters and given the opportunity to develop editorial skills.

For part of one year, I was away from the programme taking the Aotearoa Broadcasting System bid for the third television channel to the Broadcasting Tribunal (see chapter 19). On my return for *Te Karere*'s fourth year I pressed again for change. I put forward a plan to increase the programme to 15 minutes a night and to develop a Maori language current affairs programme.

Ric Carlyon, the acting controller of news and current affairs, appeared receptive. He asked about additional costs and staff, but my plan didn't seek any increases. I was disappointed to learn, towards the end of 1986, that *Te Karere* would be extended in 1987, but only by one minute. I learned this from a cyclostyled form from a scheduling clerk asking me to confirm that I could deliver the extended programme in the new year. The clerk's office was across town in another building. Mr Carlyon's office was one floor above our room. Once again, we were reminded of the lack of Pakeha respect for Maori matters.

This, along with one or two other recent events, convinced me that there was no immediate prospect for meaningful advances for *Te Karere* or any other Maori language and cultural programme. I decided to retire from the field.

I had taken *Te Karere* from a frantic four minutes a night, to a news programme which, though still too short, was credible in Maori eyes. Nightly, in a natural way, the Maori language was being used to discuss the events of the day. For the first time, Maori people were being informed of events relevant to them, and from their perspective.

I didn't regularly watch *Te Karere* after I left, and paid scant attention to people who said the programme had changed. However, when I have watched it recently, I have been disappointed. It takes time to build up skills and experience, and Television New Zealand's monocultural recruiting practices have left it without experienced Maori staff. Unfortunately, Maori people are having to pay the price for that lack. While present *Te Karere* staff are trying hard, they often miss the boat, and fail to cover events on the day they happen. The programme has developed a 'tribal' nature, with reporters from a particular tribe apparently the only ones who produce stories related to that tribe.

There appears to be no Maori advocate in television. There has been no increase in *Te Karere*'s time in the last three years, apart from a meaningless headline service just before midday, and an equally meaningless (subtitled) headline service late in the evening. Once again, the subtitles satisfy a Pakeha audience using funds that might have been used to extend the Maori service. And while they have gained subtitles, the material presented is of so little substance that it tends to trivialise Maori news. The lack of real journalistic experience shows.

Te Karere was once the cutting edge of Maori language programming on New Zealand television, and the pressures that it brought to bear probably brought about other changes too. However, compliant appointments made by Television New Zealand and Radio New Zealand in the mid-'80s have served neither Maoridom nor the broadcasting services well.

The Maori Department in Television New Zealand is simply not performing, despite massive injections of government money. *Te Karere* too is performing poorly. In my view, they are failing because the people running them have been unable to stand up to their Pakeha directors, the same people who have failed to deliver programmes suitable for Maori audiences for the last three decades.

There is no real hope for an equitable and just place for Maori language and culture in broadcasting until an independent and autonomous Maori system is established. And that system deserves the same start-up funding and opportunities enjoyed by the Pakeha broadcasting systems, Radio New Zealand and Television New Zealand.

Chapter 14

THE MEDIA AND THE WAITANGI TRIBUNAL: THE NGAI TAHU EXPERIENCE

Tipene O'Regan

The Ngai Tahu claim hearings before the Waitangi Tribunal opened on the Tuahiwi marae north of Christchurch in September 1987. The Tribunal's report is expected in March 1990. Te Ngai Tahu claim comprises nine different claims and a lot of what the Ngai Tahu counsel, Paul Temm, QC, describes as 'undergrowth'. These claims cover the bulk of the South Island, and they have been brought against all crown land within the Ngai Tahu tribal area — the biggest of any Maori tribal community.

The area has within it Christchurch and Dunedin with their three city newspapers and a wide crop of provincial and small-town papers. There are two Television New Zealand newsrooms — one each in Christchurch and Dunedin — and a number of vigorous commercial radio stations ranging in size from Ashburton and Gore to the active Christchurch market. As well as the southern regional media, we've also warranted the attention of national television, the national press and the monthly magazine sector. All of this adds up to a potentially rich crop of commentary and reporting on what Ngai Tahu are up to and the deliberations of the Tribunal itself.

While this drawn-out case has trundled on before the Tribunal, there have also been various High Court actions brought on Maori fishing rights and state asset sales, and other cases heard under Town and Country Planning laws. The Tribunal's reports on the Muriwhenua fisheries claims, Orakei, Waiheke and the Mangonui sewage case entered this whirlpool of Maori legal activity. All this generated a strong public response. Debate was sometimes intense, and our parliamentarians got into the act with a vengeance. Much of the debate centred on the role, function and competence of the Tribunal. Through it all, the Tribunal sat steadfastly through the Ngai Tahu claim hearings.

When we set out on the claim journey in 1986, Ngai Tahu went to a lot of trouble to explain to the media just what the case was about. We held press conferences and obtained the assistance of one of the country's most respected journalists to advise us on management of our media relations. We published several thousand copies of a book on the claims and have since published another. We held briefing seminars explaining that we wanted to communicate to our fellow New Zealanders what the case was about and why they didn't need to panic.

Did all this work? Is the view of the Tribunal process and our case any more informed than it was in 1986? Has all the wider debate and coverage about the

Treaty helped or hindered that understanding we set out to achieve? More importantly, is the public comprehension of the Tribunal and its role in resolving our differences really any greater for all the debate?

The major task the media assumes is reporting what it decides is news. What should be reported and how it should be reported is decided by the media themselves. Consumers have virtually no quality control on the content of news and current events material fed to them. The marvellous thing is how little they complain about the diet.

There is a built-in disposition towards 'bad' or disturbing news in the selection process and a resistance to 'positive' or 'good' news. It is much easier, for instance, to secure extensive coverage of a report which reveals some scandalous misuse of public funds by a Maori enterprise than of a brilliantly successful job-producing scheme in which every cent is properly accounted for. If a Waitangi Tribunal case involves disturbance of, or indeed merely threatens to disturb, existing property rights of Pakeha, then that's news — especially for television and radio. There is little interest in why the case has been brought or the roots of the injustice lying behind the claim. Emphasis is placed on the present conflict, which inevitably puts the responsibility for raising the issue on the complainant. The injured party thus becomes the cause of the problem.

To be fair to the electronic media, their nature necessitates brevity. There just isn't time for a news story to do much more than report unhappiness or stress, or to quote the loudest voices of complaint. Current events backgrounders in other parts of their programmes offer more information. Radio is a more relaxed and less costly medium than television so it delivers more of this sort of information. Television is both very costly and subject to intense competition for air time. Unless an issue is really 'on the boil' it has little chance of being given time for balanced analysis on air, no matter how important it is.

Newspapers extend their news reporting in editorials and in less prominent reports and commentaries. The print medium has more opportunity to publish commentary and analysis, but is still ultimately driven by the currency of a subject, and is little better at handling long-running issues. Television and radio have a far greater impact on public consciousness. They shape public opinion more rapidly and directly, and they usually get the first opportunity to cover a story, albeit in a brutally compressive way.

Once an idea has been set on its track in the public mind, all that follows in backgrounders and detail tends to be shaped by that initial view. If it is bad news, then the backgrounder sets out to explain either why it's not so bad or why things are, in fact, worse. This process of adjustment deals poorly with complex subjects and those which require some sense of history or cultural perspective. A high level of journalistic skill is needed to strip such topics down to fit into radio and television formats. On the whole, we don't have a wealth of such skills in our news media.

All of this places the Tribunal and Treaty issues at a disadvantage. The nature of the process of which the Tribunal is a central part — the orderly resolution of historical injustice — is slow. It is unsuited to the rush and bustle of newsrooms. There's no time for explaining the history. It's hard for the media to hold public interest in cases that take months or even years, as in the Ngai Tahu case. The temptation to sensationalise or to exaggerate in order to capture viewer or reader attention is enormous.

Given these problems inherent in media handling of Tribunal and Treaty issues, it is perhaps remarkable that coverage has been as good as it has. The same cannot be said for the media's handling of wider race relations issues or its coverage of Maori events or political debate involving Maori. Neither can it be said that the performance is even across all media. What can be said is that the New Zealand media have not as yet descended to the 'race crisis, armed revolution' scare-mongering that has typified Australian media coverage of New Zealand issues in recent years.

Media handling of claims to the Tribunal has two aspects. First, the Tribunal itself is described and examined; secondly, the Tribunal proceedings and the argument surrounding a particular case are reported. Over the period the Ngai Tahu case has been running, there have been substantial attacks on the Tribunal process as a way of resolving Treaty issues and on the actual competence and operation of the Tribunal. These attacks were loudest in mid-1988, with the formation of the One New Zealand Foundation attracting extensive media coverage. Criticism of marae venues for Waitangi Tribunal hearings featured in parliamentary debate and among the anti-Tribunal lobby. The Tribunal responded by shifting its Ngai Tahu claim venues to 'neutral' locations. Senior politicians eventually rose to the defence of the Tribunal, and their response was extensively covered.

Generally, editorial coverage of the debate has been balanced and fair, a significant proportion actually supportive. A major *North and South* article on the Tribunal had an impact beyond the magazine's readership and became a source for other commentators and reporters. Similarly, a substantial four-part series in the *National Business Review* focused attention on the work of the Tribunal in a positive way. Feature articles in the metropolitan daily press, noticeably the Christchurch *Press*, set out to explain the membership and workings of the Tribunal. Overall, the effect was non-threatening and positive. The exception to this generally positive media approach has been television, which has yet to give significant coverage to the Tribunal or its work beyond reporting, from time to time, Tribunal decisions or proceedings.

In my view, the public, particularly in the south, have had considerable opportunity to learn about the nature and work of the Tribunal. There have been numerous opportunities to attend hearings, invitations frequently being extended by the media. Those who plead ignorance now have only themselves to blame.

Treatment and coverage of the Ngai Tahu claim proceedings, though, have been another matter. As the biggest case to come before the Tribunal to date, one would have expected it to merit national coverage. In fact, the national parks element of the case barely got beyond the *Southland Times*, and the south Canterbury water issues beyond the *Timaru Herald*. Comparable issues north of the Bombay Hills would have been imposed on the whole nation by television, radio and the metropolitan dailies as a result of the domination of national news by the media concentration in Auckland. If they're happening in a remote and unserviced part of New Zealand, events tend to merit little media attention.

One newspaper, however, the Christchurch *Press*, has covered every sitting of the Tribunal within Te Waipounamu, and it has reported the case faithfully, though even the *Press* has shown less interest when the Tribunal has moved beyond Canterbury to Otago, Southland or the West Coast.

Newspapers in smaller provincial centres have reported Tribunal proceedings fairly when the Tribunal has sat locally, but almost entirely ignored it when it has sat elsewhere. Recent hearings in Christchurch have included material of vital importance to Southland and Otago, but those regions have been completely deprived of this information. Radio and television have largely ignored the content of the case, perhaps because its complexity makes compact coverage difficult.

Not impossible though, as has been proved by the Australian ABC radio and SBS television networks, which have both produced extensive features on the Ngai Tahu case that have demonstrated balance and careful research. In contrast, Television New Zealand's *Koha* programme and *EyeWitness* have both produced rather limited, superficial features.

Probably the most effective public education on the content of the case has been achieved through the sale and distribution of thousands of copies of the two books about the Ngai Tahu claims published by the Ngai Tahu Maori Trust Board. Distributed widely in Te Waipounamu — in schools, homes and libraries — they are often referred to and will be around long after transitory television images and radio announcements are forgotten. The second volume was first published by the *Press* as a series of leader articles over a period of several weeks in order to balance a parallel series by writers hostile to Treaty issues and critical of the interest in them.

On the whole, Ngai Tahu feel they've been fairly treated by the print media in their own region. The fact that they've been largely ignored, misreported or misunderstood by the press in other regions is basically a reflection of New Zealand parochialism.

News journalists approach societal conflict with the zest of seagulls around the tip. It is in the nature of their calling that they feed the tensions too. Their more critical colleagues, the commentators, feature writers and editorialists, tend to serve the Treaty and our understanding better. Increased public understanding of the Treaty, the Waitangi Tribunal and related issues will come about slowly through a gradual change in perceptions rather than revelation.

Chapter 15
OVERSTAYERS: A CASE OF EXAGGERATION
Prue Toft

This chapter examines media coverage of the 'overstayer' issue in the years 1974–76 and 1986–88. These periods have been selected because various factors contributed to make overstaying a public issue in those years. Of particular interest is the role of the media in shaping public opinion, in representing the issues in a balanced and sensitive manner, and in influencing the degree of racial antagonism in the community.

1974–1976: dawn raids and random checking

In March of 1974, the Prime Minister, Norman Kirk, was reported in the *New Zealand Herald* as saying that curbs on immigration might be necessary if our economic resources, particularly housing, were 'strained too severely'. While this remark referred particularly to British migrants, Pacific visitors, who had been an asset to the workforce in more prosperous times, now found themselves less welcome in the worsening economic climate.

Acting on information from the Immigration Division of the Department of Labour, the police undertook a campaign of seeking out, convicting and deporting visitors from Tonga, Western Samoa and Fiji who had overstayed their permits. The method of enforcement came to be known as 'dawn raids' as the police sought to surprise suspected offenders by early-morning checks. A prominent Tongan lawyer described this procedure in the *Herald* (19/3/74). The family he was defending had been woken at 1.00 a.m. by police officers and, when they were unable to locate their passports immediately, had been taken into police custody until proof of their residential status could be provided. Ten days later a *Herald* headline announced 'Warrants Out for Islanders'. The article stated that arrest warrants for nine Tongan and one Samoan overstayer had been issued. And the following day the *Herald* headline 'Tongans Must Go Tomorrow' referred to the deportation of five Tongan people.

In 1975, the National Party election campaign provoked protests for adopting racist advertising directed against migrants. A television broadcast contained a cartoon depicting a Polynesian character snarling and clawing the air like a tiger, then fighting with a Pakeha. The narrator warned that Labour policies had caused unemployment, which in turn aroused anger and violence, 'especially among those who came from other places expecting great things'.

An investigating officer from the Race Relations Office saw the National Party as 'climbing on the bandwagon of Polynesian violence'. She felt that the cartoon obviously referred to Polynesians, and that the implication was that Polynesians are violent people, or more correctly, are involved in the violence on our streets. More importantly, however, the featuring of a Polynesian-type figure only in a violent situation, in the light of the adverse, negative publicity relating to Polynesians and violence, has the net effect of stereotyping Polynesians as violent people.[1]

In a 1976 *New Zealand Monthly Review* editorial, further criticism was made of the manipulation of public attitudes for political gain.

During the recent election campaign, the National Party went to great pains to make immigration a major issue. In the process it was guilty of the most grave distortions and thoroughly dishonest appeals to latent racism in the New Zealand population.

There is nothing new, of course, in times of economic difficulty, in blaming 'migrants' for shortages of housing, social services, hospital facilities and employment and other breakdowns in the system. There is undoubtedly a good case for saying that in such times, at least, further immigration is going to compound such problems. However, what was completely uncalled for in the National Party's campaign was the deliberate attempt to place the blame on Pacific Island migrants.[2]

The random checking of Pacific Island people's passports received considerable publicity in 1976, owing in particular to statements from a senior police officer which were widely reported in the media. He had advised that 'a person who does not look and sound like a New Zealander' was likely to be stopped and checked for valid permits, and went on to state: 'It would be helpful to us and them if Pacific Islanders carried passports during this period.'[3]

Anti-racist groups likened this policy to South Africa's pass laws, as it gave licence to apprehend non-Europeans in public places. Reports suggested not only that legitimate Pacific Island residents and New Zealand Maori were subjected to these indignities, but that overstayers from Europe and North America were exempted from such treatment. After public criticism, it was decided that the police needed to clarify and tighten up their procedures.

Following this period, the weight of public opinion against such enforcement techniques, coupled with more effective administrative control over immigration, saw an end to these more extreme investigation procedures. Another 10 years were to pass before this issue achieved a comparable media profile.

1986–1988: abolition of visas

In 1986, an *Auckland Star* journalist, David McLoughlan, completed an investigation of Immigration Division records that revealed disturbing trends in overstayer prosecution and deportation. He opened his *Sunday Star* report of 23 March 1986 with the statement 'Immigration officers practise racial discrimination in the search for and prosecution of overstayers.' On 12 August 1986, the *Auckland Star* ran a front-page story under the headline 'Race Conciliator Backs Our Story'. His findings, later confirmed by a report from the Race Relations Office, indicated that although Tongan, Fijian and Samoan people constituted about a third of the country's overstayers, they represented 86 percent of prosecutions under the

Immigration Act 1964. Visitors from North America and the United Kingdom also represented about a third of the overstaying population, but only 5.1 percent of these nationalities were prosecuted for the same offence. It appeared that Immigration Division policy and procedures focused on particular ethnic groups.

A defence of this policy from the division argued that these ethnic groups were known to be long-term overstayers, while offenders from the United Kingdom, North America and elsewhere would depart voluntarily without the need for legal intervention. Once more, David McLoughlan was able to produce evidence which showed Tongans, Fijians and Samoans did not have substantially different overstaying patterns from other visitors. Most overstayers, irrespective of nationality, overstay for less than 12 months.

As this challenge to Immigration Division practices was raised by a journalist, the debate had a high media profile in 1986. McLoughlan proposed that because the Immigration Division perceived Pacific Island people to be the most likely group to overstay, they pursued policies that made their detection and apprehension more easily achieved than other visitors'. In particular, Tongan, Samoan and Fijian visitors were required to have visas while other travellers were not, and closer records were maintained on their whereabouts.

Not only were official policies reported to discriminate against these Pacific Islanders, but informal practices also operated to their disadvantage. Endless queuing, unclear instructions and disrespectful attitudes were often mentioned in the context of contact with officials. The *Auckland Star* (15/4/86) reported that a Tongan couple who wished to attend their daughter's graduation in Auckland had their visa application denied because the house of the relatives with whom they planned to stay was too small. When another relative offered accommodation in his six-bedroomed house, immigration officers raised a new problem — another daughter would have to return home, they said, before the parents would be permitted into the country. Then the immigration officer lost their forms. The reporter commented:

> If Pacific Islanders and Indians have problems, North Americans, Europeans and Australians do not. They don't need any visa. Australians don't even need a passport. Nobody asks them about the number of bedrooms or says their daughters must go home before they are allowed in. Their forms are not lost or filled out wrongly because none are needed.

Recommendations that arose from this inquiry were embodied in the Immigration Bill 1986. In particular it was proposed

- that visitors from Tonga, Fiji and Samoa should no longer need visas, as other nationalities were not obliged to produce them;
- that the offence of overstaying be decriminalised; and
- that an offender should have right of re-entry after five years, where previously they were barred for life.

It was announced that from December 1986 Tongan, Western Samoan and Fijian visitors could enter New Zealand for three months without visas. This policy had applied to Western Europeans, Japanese and North Americans since 1985.

In early February 1987, the *Herald* ran the headline 'Visa Office Rush by Islanders', and exorbitant figures were broadcast about the number of Samoan and Tongan people entering the country. The *Herald* published a cartoon on 19 February 1987 depicting grinning caricatures of people from the Pacific Islands bursting through a door the Minister of Immigration attempts to push shut, while the Prime Minister shouts, 'Shut the door, they're coming through the window.' As the new school year began, newpaper headlines suggested the education system was facing chaos because of mass enrolment by Pacific Island students who could not speak English. Some principals, however, were drawn to inform the media that they welcomed these students.

The visa exemption was abolished in February 1987 when it was considered that an insupportable number of people had entered New Zealand under the scheme. An *Auckland Star* editorial (25/2/87) called for a calmer approach to the situation. It was observed that 'thousands' of European visitors entered the country under the same conditions and that it was unwarranted to assume that these Pacific Island people were overstaying since the three-month visiting period had not even expired when the scheme was abolished. Immigration Division officials were admonished for using figures that were more than double the actual number of visitors.

In the months that followed, the media took a moderate line. In the *Star* (16/4/87), it was suggested that the unexpected response of visitors was caused partly by a rumour circulated in Tonga that the visa exemption was a temporary measure. In Western Samoa, unusually low airfares, coupled with the increased Pacific Island travel that would be expected for the holiday period, had contributed to the situation. By the end of 1987, attention was focused on the Immigration Division's difficulties in dealing with large numbers of people who sought to take advantage of the amnesty, and those who required more general services. On 18 May 1988, the *Herald* reported that applicants were sleeping in cars and on the pavement overnight to secure a place in the queue. Two days later the *Star* reported that people were spending up to three days in the queue. There were also suggestions that 'Islanders' had been misled to believe that registration under the amnesty implied residency would be automatically granted. As the amnesty came to an end, in December 1988, the media began to warn once more of a 'crackdown' on overstayers, indicating the liberal attitudes had been short term.

Conclusion

The media have played two different roles in the debate over overstaying. In the periods reviewed, the public has been presented with media items that suggest all Pacific Island people have a tendency to overstay. In fact, Cook Islanders, Tokelauans and Niueans have legitimate residency rights in New Zealand, while Western Samoans, Fijians and Tongans have been unjustly identified as overstaying more frequently than visitors from Europe and North America. Media reporting has helped associate Pacific Islanders with 'overstaying', which in turn has been defined as a social problem.

But conversely, the media have also aroused public indignation against dawn raids and random checking and have rigorously challenged the Immigration

Division's practices and policies. David McLoughlan's reporting has been of particular significance in recent years.

In conclusion, it could be said that the media have both reflected and shaped social attitudes towards Pacific migrants. It is no accident that stereotypes of non-European overstaying and wrongdoing have been so readily absorbed by the community. New Zealand has had a long and ignoble history of prejudice against migrants who failed to conform to the colonial 'white New Zealand' policy.

In many instances, the media are dependent on information from 'expert' sources, and at times this has been misleading — for example, when the Immigration Division justified its pursuit of Pacific Island offenders. But in recent years, some sections of the media have challenged government departments on their treatment of Pacific Island overstayers. This has helped alert the public to the racism of particular departments. The media have therefore exercised power, at different times, both to represent more conservative Pakeha interests and to raise public consciousness in the interests of greater social justice for migrants.

Chapter 16

THE MAORI LOANS AFFAIR AND THE MEDIA'S SCANDAL MENTALITY

Vern Rice

It was Christmas 1986, the silly season, when the whole country closes down and the media are desperate for any kind of story. Then along came the sort of scandal that any metropolitan news organisation would kill for. Suddenly, television, radio and the newspapers were leading with the story which was quickly dubbed the 'Maori loans affair' and involved attempts by the Maori Affairs Department to borrow a large sum of money privately (and, as it turned out, improperly).

The news coverage revolved around a number of questions — some explicit, some implicit. Among them: How did the loan negotiations get so far? Which heads will roll? Who is this character Max Raepple? Is Koro Wetere in line for the boot? But underpinning the public and media interest was another, implicit question: What the hell are these Maoris up to?

In retrospect, the Maori loans affair was attractive to New Zealand's journalists, chief reporters and news editors in all sorts of ways. It conjured up visions of secret meetings with foreign middlemen in smoke-filled rooms, with a West German financier of dubious repute, millions of dollars from Arab sources, and a Government hell-bent on buying the whole sorry mess and shielding the guilty parties. At the end of it all, when the public bloodletting was over, Maori people and Maori initiatives had been seriously compromised.

Very briefly then, the Maori Affairs Minister, Koro Wetere, had appointed Rotorua businessman Rocky Cribb to act as agent in Hawaii, where Cribb initiated loan negotiations on the department's behalf. The Secretary of Maori Affairs, Tamati Reedy, assumed total control of the negotiations in November 1986. He was advised early that month by Treasury Secretary Graham Scott to investigate the source of the proposed $600 million loan, and told that only the Minister of Finance could authorise such a transaction. Towards the end of November, the Minister ordered Dr Reedy to stop the loan negotiations and cancelled his trip to Hawaii. Meanwhile Dr Reedy had already signed a procurement fee for a Hawaiian middleman and had written to a West German financier, Max Raepple, to arrange a meeting with him in Hawaii to discuss the loan. The news got out on 16 December, when Opposition Maori Affairs spokesperson Winston Peters raised the matter in Parliament.

The media's handling of the affair has been condemned as racist by a number of Maori commentators. Despite the relative liberalism which prevails among reporters in many of the nation's newsrooms, the industry as a whole, like many others, has its fair share of the less tolerant. There were those who saw in the Maori loans affair legitimation for their critical views of Maori initiatives generally, and the bias was reflected in the way the stories were written and told, where they were placed in a bulletin or on the news page, the headlines used, and so on.

Naturally there was no way reporters and their bosses could have ignored the loans affair or relegated it to the back page. It was a news item of great public interest. What, for example, would have been the result if the $600 million loan had gone through? Could it have been cancelled once the deal was signed? Would Maori land have been used as collateral? How could an economically impoverished people have been expected to pay the sum back, plus interest, even at 4 percent? Yet it's hard to avoid the conclusion that if a Pakeha department and its public servants were caught up in a similar débâcle, the storm would quickly blow over; it is certainly highly unlikely they would suffer the fallout for years afterwards. This was the lot reserved for a minority group with no power in the media, little influence in the Government and limited access to expert advice in matters of finance.

The Maori Affairs Department, indeed all Maori people, have paid a heavy price over the loans affair, and continue to pay it. It came at a time when Maori economic development was really starting to take off, and it provided a ready excuse for the Government to intervene in an effort to shape Maori progress according to its own rules. The 'scandal' revealed the paternalism of the Government and a widespread fear among Pakeha of the Maori drive for autonomy. Many Maori people cynically await the day when news headlines will scream 'Pakeha Work Trust Scandal Revealed' or 'Pakeha Loan Scam Condemned by Audit Office'.

The media's scandal mode can often cause personal hurt. Typical are the shock/horror probes featuring the public servant/work trust/mother-of-three who spent $10,000 of taxpayers' money and got away with it. These may include interviews with incensed Opposition MPs, distraught/defiant parents and/or embarrassed business associates. The stories impact humiliatingly on alleged Pakeha miscreants as well as Maori.

The reporters of these stories and their editors must ensure that the need for the disclosure of a potential financial impropriety involving public funds is not merely used as an excuse for a hard-hitting front-page story that provides a great headline on the billboard. Often the appetite for a sensational story predominates. As a result, people's names and alleged misdemeanours are bandied about with apparent impunity. Later, when the dust settles, and it perhaps emerges that some charges against them were excessive or incorrect, some of the dirt inevitably sticks anyway.

Maori feel keenly the hypocrisy of the front-page attention given, say, to the Maori trust which has failed to produce its accounts, when the Government escapes similar table-thumping indignation over the hundreds of millions of dollars it wastes annually through inefficiency in, say, the hospital system.

These issues will not vanish in a hurry. As private enterprises, mainstream media organisations resist public accountability. Trumpeting their editorial independence, they will be Pakeha dominated for decades to come. Separate Maori media outlets, offering Maori news in a Maori way, provide the best hope in the near future for combating the negative, monocultural orientation of mainstream news services. Non-Maori converts are likely to be picked up along the way.

In the meantime, Maori need to learn to play the Pakeha-dominated media at their own game, developing their own publication strategies, cultivating good relationships with journalists, and becoming proactive, promoting positive news about their enterprises, instead of always reacting to scandal-seeking newshounds. This active approach does not necessarily guarantee great press — even the smoothest public relations companies do not always win the war of media manipulation — but it certainly beats always being on the receiving end.

Chapter 17

AN INCIDENT IN OTARA: THE MEDIA AND PACIFIC ISLAND COMMUNITIES

Finau 'Ofa Kolo

Media coverage of Pacific Island news and events is usually inadequate and tends to reinforce a negative image of Pacific Islanders, who are regularly portrayed in the pages of New Zealand dailies and weeklies as criminals, overstayers, rapists, unemployed dole bludgers, streetbrawlers, and so on. Rarely are there positive stories about Pacific Islanders to balance these images.

Media interest in Pacific Island communities in New Zealand goes back to the early 1970s. This was the era when news about Pacific Islanders and their communities came to the fore because of a widespread perception, shared and contributed to by the media, that Pacific Island migrants were a 'problem'. It is significant that the first extensive media coverage of Pacific Islanders led to the creation of negative stereotypes. This was the period of 'dawn raids', when Pacific Island homes were raided by New Zealand police and immigration officials searching for overstayers.

The extensive coverage by the media of the overstaying issue consequently led to the creation of a widely held stereotype of Pacific Islanders as overstayers and illegal immigrants. Recently, this stereotype was disputed by *Auckland Star* journalist David McLoughlan and the Office of the Race Relations Conciliator. A study by the *Auckland Star* journalist, which was later verified by the investigations of the Race Relations Office, found that overstayers from other countries far outnumbered those from the Pacific Islands, but that more than 80 percent of those apprehended and prosecuted were Pacific Islanders. Despite such findings, for most, the word 'overstayer' remains firmly associated with the Pacific Islander. This negative image is reinforced by the attention that the media give to 'disorder' events involving Pacific Islanders. A case in point is the 1989 incident involving Samoans and Tongans in Otara.

On Saturday morning, 30 April 1989, during the peak hours of trading at the very popular Otara fleamarket, a group of Samoan youths killed a Tongan man and seriously injured another. Media reaction to the incident was immediate. For the next eight months or so, the incident (and related stories) featured frequently in Auckland dailies and weeklies. Many stories went nationwide.

Considering the brutality of the crime, the media had a right and responsibility to inform the public of the event. It is not the publishing of the stories as such that should concern us; it is the obsession with which this negative event was reported and the way it was handled.

Stories about the incident were published on the front pages of the Auckland papers, with bold headlines making direct reference to Samoans and Tongans. Banner headlines such as 'Samoans appear in packed courtroom', 'Samoan searching for "pride"',[1] and 'Tongan men "planning own attack"'[2] cast the event as inter-ethnic conflict. Ninety percent of those named in the stories relating to the incident were ethnically tagged — that is, the people were explicitly described as Samoan or Tongan. About 80 percent of the story intros specifically mentioned the ethnicity of the accused or the victims.

Ethnic tagging is a major feature in media reports only when the subjects of those reports are not members of the majority culture. Two questions need to be asked regarding this issue. Why is the tagging of minority ethnic groups so extensively used? Is it relevant to the media's coverage? (See chapter 5.)

It took three days for an accurate and factual story to be printed.[3] One of the two writers of this story, Fetuli Ioane, is a Pacific Islander who was then a journalism trainee at Manukau Polytechnic. The story, 'What really happened in Otara', which featured on the front page of the *Auckland Star* was very critical of preceding coverage of the incident. The earlier material inaccurately explained the incident as resulting from a gang feud. The other media myth which the two writers helped to dispel was that the killing was a consequence of a 'race war' between Samoans and Tongans. And the piece went on to tell of the anger of Pacific Islanders at the way the print media had drawn up its headlines and covered the event.

The story was well researched and uncovered new information. It deserved the award it gained as runner-up in the New Zealand Foundation for Peace Studies media awards. In considering stories for the award, judges looked at integrity and balance, as opposed to sensationalism. Mr Ioane and his co-writer, Karen Mangnall, carefully and thoroughly explored the events which led to the killing and helped dispel the idea that there was a 'race war' between Tongans and Samoans. In this, Mr Ioane demonstrated the strength of being a journalist and a Pacific Islander.

During the period of the incident's media exposure and the aftermath (for example, community attempts to resolve the problem, court proceedings, and so on), other activities in the Pacific Island communities were simply ignored. Important cultural festivals and events which took place during this period apparently did not match the murder incident for sensationalism.

The media's coverage of the Otara conflict was very damaging to the Pacific Island communities, especially those which were directly involved. The extensive reporting of the murder incident and the consequent court proceedings, along with the constant identification and association of the incident with the Pacific Island communities involved, meant that stereotypical views of Pacific Islanders were further reinforced.

The media's unbalanced and inconsistent or insensitive reporting concerns an increasing number of Pacific Islanders. The Otara affair was blown up out of all proportion. The New Zealand public was told that the killing was gang-related, and that it was part of a 'race war' between Samoans and Tongans which could be traced back to pre-contact times. The many community attempts to resolve the problem, though noted in the media, were given much less attention than stories of the incident and court proceedings. The image of Otara as an unsafe place to live because its population is predominantly Polynesian was strengthened.

In order to report accurately, sensitively and responsibly Pacific Island concerns and events, the media must anticipate the possible consequences of their coverage. Reporters and editors must appreciate cultural differences. By doing this, the media will enjoy the hospitality of Pacific Island people and will be better placed to provide a more balanced view of their activities to the wider public.

Chapter 18

TALES OF TERROR IN PALMERSTON NORTH

Gordon Campbell

There are street kids in Palmerston North terrorising the public — or so some people would say. But behind the sensational headlines a very different story emerges.

No one really loves a flat city, so, all things considered, the Square in Palmerston North is a good attempt at making up for what nature forgot to provide. But that's 'Parmy' for you. The city has grown through sheer grit and effort, and the sense of 'didn't we do well' is obvious. 'Been long since you were here last?' asks the taxi-driver on the way in from the airport. 'Gone ahead, hannit?'

But right now, times are tough. The media are treating Palmerston North as if it were Beirut. 'Child terror gangs' stalk the streets, says the *8 O'Clock* newspaper. The city is being held to ransom, says the *Dominion*, by a gang of juvenile glue-sniffing thugs. Juvenile? According to the *Dominion* the gang that 'gloatingly' calls itself the Highbury Hoods has members who are only four years old!

Later in the afternoon, I met the Highbury Hoods up at the Highbury shopping centre. There are about 15 or 16 of them: some are Maori, some are Pakeha. They're on their way to rugby league practice. Despite the tales of glue sniffing, they look healthy and well fed. None has that peaky, strung-out look common among the so-called 'street kids' of Auckland and Wellington. Ho Chi, their youngest member, is 13.

They'd like to see a community centre in Highbury. Some place where they could go to play sport, to run a disco some nights . . . to, y'know, just get together with their mates. 'What're kids like in Wellington?' one young girl asks wistfully. 'What do they like to do on weekends?' The glue? The stores have cracked down and made it hard to get. They're going off it anyhow. Was big around December, January, but not now. (This decline in the glue problem to a hard core of 20 to 30 kids spread across the entire city was confirmed by Sue Neill of the police youth aid division.)

The publicity? Some like it, try to live up to it; some think it's been 'all bullshit'. 'We're not violent,' one says quietly. 'If we were violent we wouldn't even talk to you.'

The Highbury kids are not street kids, says Laurence Mepham, a community youth worker with the city council. Most live at home, or stay for periods at

This article first appeared in the Listener *(3/8/85). Though the events described occurred five years ago, it is included here for the light it sheds on how media myths are created. The present abridged version is reproduced with the kind permission of the author, the* Listener *and the Highbury Whanau.*

homes run by adults elsewhere in the community. 'If you've got kids who go to school or to the Steps programme, who come home on the bus to have a feed, who hang around with their mates and then go home again . . . they're not street kids.'

Street children. Kids at risk. Whatever you call them, they've been part of New Zealand life for at least 118 years. As long ago as 1867, police were granted power under the Neglected and Criminal Children's Act to take into custody without warrant any children 'wandering about or frequenting any street, thoroughfare, tavern or place of public resort or sleeping in the open air'.

Palmerston North's troubles don't go back quite that far, but they certainly did not begin with the Highbury Hoods. In the early 1980s, there were the 'bridge kids' allegedly living under the Fitzherbert Street bridge. Then there were the 'fire station kids' living in a disused downtown fire station. Civic leaders had ample warning of Highbury's own needs. In 1983 a city council survey of suburban recreational needs reported: 'Highbury has a large number of young people and any future development must take into account the needs of Highbury's young population.' The current publicity will probably make it harder to rally any community or business support to satisfy those needs. Among the more blatant distortions:

Dominion June 19: 'A glue-sniffing teenager intentionally vomited on the lap of an elderly bus passenger. . . . There has been the threatening and intentional vomiting on elderly bus passengers.'
Fact: No such vomiting has occurred. The city bus driver's report to bus manager John Galbraith shows on May 23 one elderly bus passenger was spat at.

Dominion June 19: 'A young thug handed over a concession card held in the palm of his hand. As the driver went to take it he noticed it was lying on top of a vicious strop razor the thug had produced from his sleeve.'
Fact: No such incident occurred, says Galbraith. A razor was found in a rubbish tin on a city bus. Some time ago a youth did brandish a knife on a bus, but the incident was not deemed worth including in the driver's report. In the main, reported behaviour involved swearing, playing radios loudly, glue sniffing, avoiding fares and riding in the luggage racks.

Dominion June 19: 'A group of young hoodlums thrown out of the police-run blue light disco retaliated by breaking into the Civic Centre, defecating on the mayor's desk and smashing $20,000 worth of computer equipment.'
Fact: The police file shows that the mayor's office was not broken into, much less his desk defecated on. A secretary's desk nearby was written on, the woman concerned told me. All but $5,000 of the computer gear was recovered, says Detective Dave Christian. The kids stole it, he says, because they thought they could play space invaders on the video consoles. 'Pathetic, really.'

In May, Sergeant Neil Hickey warned the public about the danger of robbery or assault in the square at night. The Highbury kids were responsible, according to the *Dominion*. 'The gang terrorises Highbury during the week and then moves its activities to the Square on Friday and Saturday nights.'

Acting police commander Mick Tarling disagrees. Highbury kids may have been involved in some anti-social behaviour in the square, but the assaults and so forth were caused by other young people who had been drinking in clubs and hotels and came into the square late at night. 'The first thing we identified was that it wasn't the kids from Highbury.' With a 'minimum of publicity' extra patrols on hotels and drink/driving checks had now had a 'positive' impact on the problems in the square.

Is Palmerston North really in the grip of a crime wave? According to the *Dominion*, a record number of burglaries occurred during the first 17 days of June. The city is a 'burglar's paradise', according to the *Evening Standard*.

In fact, the city had 175 burglaries in June — only six more than the average for January, February and March. During the first quarter of 1985, 12.9 percent of burglaries were solved — not a good rate, but only 2 percent worse than the national average for the same period. How serious were the June offences? Nothing was taken in 21 of the 175 cases, and in only 42 did the property stolen exceed $1,000 in value.

Eleven of these 175 burglaries took place in the Highbury region bounded by Tremaine Avenue, Botanical Road and Pioneer Highway; and only two of the 42 serious offences occurred there, neither at the Highbury shopping centre. In other words, 6 percent of Palmerston North's burglaries in June took place in Highbury — exactly what one would expect in a suburb that, according to the 1981 census, contained 6 percent of the city's population.

The major property offences in Palmerston North are being carried out by an older age group, says Detective George Wood, and not by the Highbury kids. They, he agrees, are usually after smokes and a few lollies. Wood also discounts the widespread rumour that adult criminals are using the kids for burglaries and paying them with glue and other drugs.

One form of crime *is* rocketing in Palmerston North. Credit card offences quadrupled in the first quarter of 1985 and the problem has not lessened since then, says Wood. Most of these frauds involve multiple offences and run into 'four-figure numbers'. Needless to say, this white-collar crime wave has not received anything like the attention focused by the police and the media on the children (and parents) of Highbury.

Mick Tarling is the city's top police officer. For eight years he was the police community work co-ordinator in Christchurch, and he has been in Palmerston North for four years. In the *Dominion* he took a hard line on the street kids and their parents and commended the *Dominion* articles. But in the local newspaper he rebutted some of the *Dominion* claims and used a less sensational tone. How come?

Tarling is frank about the political game involved. 'I wanted impact. The fact was, we tended to find that different social agencies weren't, I felt, supporting what the police were trying to do. I'm talking about Social Welfare.' Maori Affairs, he later adds, was also 'taking a soft line' on young offenders. 'There's no doubt that the impact of what I've said stirred those social agencies and they're coming up positively with finance and staff when, up until a week ago, we couldn't get past the door.'

Kelvin Menzies, assistant director of social work with the Social Welfare Department in Palmerston North, says there has been no change in how his department carries out its duties. Two extra temporary staff have recently been appointed. At the same time — and this, Tarling says, explains why he might seem to be talking 'on another tangent' — he wanted to reassure local people that the problem was not a large one. Only 25 to 30 'kids at risk' among 17 000 'good kids' in the greater Manawatu area.

The publicity to date, I suggest, has stigmatised the suburb of Highbury and fuelled the fears of ordinary citizens. Parents have been made scapegoats for problems that are largely not of their making, and the Highbury shopkeepers, the kids and the wider community have been further polarised. How does this assist the goals of community policing?

'Matter of fact, it's improved them. . . . We've found over the last fortnight that the people are starting to come out around the Highbury shops in full safety.' It's going to take a while, he concedes, 'before we can see if it's something that's positive'. But he is hearing from Rotary and other organisations he belongs to that it's good to see the police being positive.

Six months ago, Tarling says, he tried the community approach. He went to two meetings up at St Michael's Hall. 'My plan of attack was to involve the community in their problem and it just didn't work.' Now, some parents tell police to 'fuck off' when they call round to houses to follow up complaints. He's aware that some parents are trying to run discos for the kids. But glue sniffing happened at one police-run disco, 'and if we're not careful that could happen with their own disco. Now is that right?'

When a suburb like Highbury lacks basic facilities for the kids, I ask Tarling, how are parents on low incomes supposed to provide them? When both parents and solo mothers have to work to make ends meet, how can they physically force their kids to stay off the street?

Tarling shrugs this off. He suggests that I have been primed by Mrs Karu, one of the Highbury parents: 'That's her speaking now.' He prefers to note the case of Reverend Hapai Winiata. 'A Maori, a minister of the church. He provides a hall, he provides everything the kids say they want. They wreck it and assault him.' (When contacted in Petone, Winiata denies this. The kids, who knew him as 'Uncle Hapai', always treated him with the 'utmost respect'. The hall sustained 'no major damage' during its months of use. The community plans shaped at the St Michael's Hall meetings fell through only because they did not meet Labour Department criteria.)

Tarling denies he has spent more time talking to the media about Highbury parents than in talking to the parents themselves. But he concedes: 'If there is a big question mark that we haven't worked on enough it would be those parents. But I spoke at both meetings on the marae and, you know, I made it clear what the police position was.'

It would cost very little to make an impact on the current needs in Highbury. The kids' rugby league and basketball teams need to be kitted out in proper uniforms — 'so that they feel like real good teams', says youth worker Laurence Mepham. Money is also needed to pay for the hire of sports venues. Mepham has plans in the pipeline to provide an outlet for the kids' artistic skills. A van is also needed to take the kids to sporting fixtures and on camping trips and other outdoor activities. Mepham has his eye on a van coming up this month in a government stores auction. To help raise the $2,000 needed, Highbury parents have, he says, run raffles and a fleamarket — but because of the adverse publicity these have not been well patronised.

In time, a community centre may emerge from a task force set up by the city's new mayor, Paul Rieger. But, Mepham warns, this will require careful planning. Such a hall will need long-term funding to maintain and supervise it. And, Mepham adds, such a hall will be successful only if both the kids and the wider community are involved from the outset. The recent publicity, he says, has made it very hard to get that kind of co-operation. But the parents' own discos have shown that the kids are ready to respond. There, the kids help with planning, run the sweet shop, play the discs and clean up afterwards.

Some Highbury parents meet regularly to share their problems and build up practical knowledge of such things as their own and their children's legal rights. The Whanau Support Group now numbers about 15 parents and they have met weekly for the last eight months with social workers, lawyers and on one occasion with Mayor Rieger. Despite the fact that community constable Ken Drake has been ready to tell the *Evening Standard* that uncaring parents are the cause of the street kid problem, Drake has never asked to meet the group. Nor has any other police officer.

The support group fiercely rejects the claim that parents don't care: 'When you've got only $5 left for groceries, what do you do?' asks Debby Green. 'You buy petrol for the car and go looking for your kid. We care all right.' They know people think they're at housie or in the pub and neglecting the children. That, they say, is untrue. After paying $120 grocery bills for their families, they couldn't do that even if they wanted to. The notion comes from a prejudice against working people, says Adrienne Baird — an attitude that links poverty with drunkenness.

People think that you can hammer discipline into kids, force them to stay home. Larry Green says he's tried and that it doesn't work. 'You hit them and you create fear, and the fear turns to hate, and then you've lost them.' Each parent has had experience of what happens at the police station when they show their concern and stand by their children. Each claims to have encountered rudeness, hostility and evasiveness from the police.

Currently, Baird says, it's a 'no win' situation. As their kids ride down the street on their bicycles or walk home from the pictures they're being stopped and searched. 'And if we leave our houses for a moment without arranging a babysitter you can come back and find the police have taken away your children.' One day, Larry Green says in exasperation, he's going to put up a poster in town: 'Today, The Police Will Catch Criminals, Not Children'.

Chapter 19

AOTEAROA BROADCASTING SYSTEM INC.

Derek Fox

The Aotearoa Broadcasting System (ABS) was the boldest and most innovative Maori effort to enter the broadcasting industry. But the idea didn't come from working broadcasters. It came from a collective of Maori people who had little practical knowledge of broadcasting, and were unaware of the enormity of the task. This group was the New Zealand Maori Council, a body often maligned by tribal groups now enjoying a renaissance, who forget that the council is the only national Maori group with a statutory obligation to our people.

The prime mover on the council was Whatarangi Winiata, professor of accounting at Victoria University, and a member of Ngati Raukawa of Otaki. Some years before, he had also been a member of the Broadcasting Corporation of New Zealand (BCNZ) board, where his persistence in representing Maori interests hadn't won him many friends, or a return term.

The Maori Council had often fruitlessly challenged the BCNZ over the poor return to its Maori shareholders. It was with those failures in mind that, in the words of chairperson Sir Graham Latimer, Maori councillors 'went for the doctor'. They empowered Professor Winiata to put together an application to seek the third channel warrants on behalf of Maoridom. He established a small working group for that purpose. It was an eleventh-hour effort which had to battle uphill and into the wind all the way.

The third channel hearings were very much a monocultural affair, and will, I believe, be held up in years to come as an example of how not to handle the disposal of a public asset in a supposedly bicultural country. The Minister of Broadcasting had asked the Broadcasting Tribunal — the distributor of broadcasting warrants — to investigate the introduction of private television to New Zealand. Rather than seek the necessary information within this country, they went overseas, and it is probably not surprising that the model they recommended was British.

It was that of Independent Television, a system of regional companies which transmit commercial television to their own patch in competition with the non-commercial BBC 1 and BBC 2 stations. The economic survival of those regional stations depends on the substantial population in each region. What seems to have escaped the Broadcasting Tribunal's notice is that the 'old country' has close to twenty times the population of New Zealand. The Tribunal's recommendations were in fact advocating three almost exclusively advertising-dependent stations to be supported by a little over 3 million people. That is something the

British still do not have despite their 60 million people.

Having made its recommendations, the Tribunal was then given the task of carrying them out. The minister, Jonathan Hunt, directed the Tribunal to call for applications for four regional warrants.

From ABS's point of view, even this starting point was contentious. The ministerial directive in no way reflected the aspirations of Maori people. Inevitably, the document reflected its author, the minister, and Mr Hunt is a hawk on Maori aspirations in broadcasting. His view is that Maori people listen to the present radio system and watch the present television system. The argument that there should be a Maori alternative did not impress him.

The climate of the Tribunal hearings was clouded by the hearings of the Royal Commission on Broadcasting, which ran parallel to the Tribunal deliberations. The royal commission caused frustration both by its timidity and its refusal to hear ABS evidence on the broad picture of how New Zealand television might be organised.

The broad picture is basically the same now. After nearly 30 years of television in New Zealand, less than 1 percent of television time is in the Maori language. After 60 years of radio in this country, and despite the 50 publicly owned radio stations broadcasting tens of thousands of hours of programmes across a range of frequencies each week, only about an hour of it is in Maori.

Television viewers here are far more likely to hear a Liverpool or New York accent than a New Zealand accent. All New Zealanders should be concerned that on their television system 80 percent of the programmes are imported. More than half of all New Zealand television is from the United States and portrays the values of that foreign society. In its best year ever, Television New Zealand raised itself to 22 percent local production.

The rationale for screening so much foreign material is that we need the revenue for more local production, but this isn't what happens. The financial rewards from transmitting foreign material are extremely high. But the cultural and social cost to New Zealand society and to Maoridom is higher still.

The cost of overseas programmes has remained constant at about $US50 a minute for a high-rating programme such as *Hill Street Blues*, for which Television New Zealand pays about $US2,500 an episode. That cost is recovered in the first advertising break in the programme. The rest is profit.

Few New Zealanders realise that in the first eight years of this decade alone, Television New Zealand and Radio New Zealand have enjoyed, through their monopoly and the public broadcasting fee, revenues of $3.4 billion — much more than the cost of four Australian frigates. Maori people have been asking what happened to their share of that bounty. Perhaps Pakeha people should start doing the same.

It was in this context that ABS got underway. A komiti whakatinana — or steering committee — was established. It comprised Professor Winiata, as chairperson, and two other members — Ariariterangi Paul, a partner with the international accounting firm Price Waterhouse, and me, a Maori broadcaster and journalist.

The hearings began with a lengthy process in which contenders submitted their applications and discussed their aspirations, and opponents were invited to challenge them. The contenders were then invited to reply to the challenges. From the beginning, ABS was the odd-applicant-out. While other contenders talked about revenue projections, whether their opponents' figures were realistic and whether each had sufficient plant or people to make the stations work, ABS sought to debate the philosophy of what was happening. We argued for the rights of Maori people to a fair share in the broadcasting system under the Treaty of Waitangi and the partnership implicit in it.

The case was simple, perhaps too simple. We pointed out that there are already two Pakeha television stations in this country: TV One and TV Two (now Channel 2). Between them, they have the opportunity to transmit the best available programmes to satisfy Pakeha needs. They make no attempt to satisfy Maori needs, and perhaps they shouldn't have to. However, before another Pakeha television station is licensed, a Maori station should be set up.

The other contenders had little or nothing to say in their original applications about Maori programming. But later almost all were to acquire Maori advisers or begin developing a 'Maori dimension'. Mostly though, their best offerings were crumbs. And as one ABS witness stated, Maori people were no longer interested in crumbs from the cake, or even a slice. What they want instead is a share in the bakery.

In order to develop, ABS needed funds, and it was Whatarangi Winiata who came up with a solution. He argued that the BCNZ used funds that should rightfully be spent on Maori broadcasting needs and that the BCNZ also owed Maoridom some back rent in this area.

Some time later, coaxed along by their former chairperson and then chief executive, Ian Cross, the BCNZ struck a deal with ABS. Basically, the deal accepted the back rent argument, and accepted the fact that, despite what Ian Cross called their best efforts, they hadn't been able to fulfil their obligations to the Maori people. The BCNZ agreed to support ABS and gave Ian Cross permission to give evidence in support before the Tribunal. The total package of support from the BCNZ included a transmission system, funding in the first three years while ABS was finding its feet in scheduling and production, and acceptance of Whatarangi Winiata's 15 percent argument. Under that arrangement, after three years, the annual television revenues would be tallied up. Should ABS have received less than 15 percent of the sum, the Maori channel funds would be topped up by Television New Zealand. Should it have received more than 15 percent, Cross's comment was, 'Good luck to you'.

ABS's principals were satisfied with their efforts. It seemed the BCNZ was willing, for its own reasons perhaps, to support the ABS arguments. Not all ABS's financial problems were solved, but it seemed logical that with the BCNZ deal in place, the remaining shortfall of funds should have been easier to overcome.

All the other third channel contenders were private companies or consortiums of major companies. Their parent companies or shareholders put up the initial finance to fight for the warrants — about $2 million each as it turned out. The investment seemed justifiable, as the successful contender could expect a considerable windfall once some shares were sold.

Share capital was an option open to ABS but rejected by the komiti whakatinana in favour of a membership system. The reason for this was to preserve the integrity of a tikanga Maori station, by avoiding a sharemarket takeover. There were three types of membership: individual at $30 per annum; corporate non-profitmaking at $100 a year; and corporate profitmaking at $1,000 a year. Only individual members could vote.

The ABS programming philosophy was to produce two-thirds of the programmes it transmitted, of which half would be in the Maori language. The remaining third of imported content would have a bias towards material produced by other tangata whenua around the world. ABS planned to generate revenues in addition to the deal with the BCNZ by screening nightly movies and other popular programmes such as sport. It is no surprise that sports and movie channels are two of the first types of new channel being set up under the new deregulated television system.

Had ABS succeeded, it would have provided a $1.5 million business, in 1985 dollar terms, in Maori ownership, provided about 500 well-paid high tech jobs, and helped Pakeha and Maori people understand each other better. But while the deal with BCNZ covered most of ABS's capital needs, it left an outstanding amount of $24 million. Compared with the rest of the picture, it didn't seem large, and we confidently began negotiations with the Bank of New Zealand. After careful study, the BNZ was satisfied with our figures and prepared to advance the money, but wanted a guarantee — not for $24 million but for only $15 million, that being the amount of the loan that would still be outstanding at the expiry of the five-year warrants.

The BCNZ declined to provide the guarantee, but suggested an approach to the Government. We went to see the Minister of Maori Affairs to inform him of the position and seek his help. It was the first of several meetings, all fruitless. The Minister had a problem. He noted, correctly, that there were Maori associated with other applications for the warrants. Indeed, elements of his own Tainui people were supporting two other contenders. It was pointed out that their involvement was small, and the programme rewards from that involvement even smaller.

Without a guarantee or any other assistance from the Government, ABS turned to Maori sources, and an approach was made to the Federation of Maori Authorities — a group comprising leaders from the Maori land blocks and trust boards around the country. The approach seemed to have borne fruit when a letter was received from the interim chairperson of the federation, Sir Hepi Te Heuheu, in which he said he would recommend to his membership that they support ABS by providing a guarantee for the $15 million.

Three days later, however, another letter arrived rescinding the first on the grounds that he had since learned that there were other Maori people with the Pakeha contenders. Significantly perhaps, a copy of the letter also went to the Minister of Maori Affairs.

For those who wanted to see, ABS had mustered considerable Maori support, much more than any other contender. There were about 2000 individual members, all of whom had paid their $30. Also there was declared support from the New Zealand Maori Council, the Maori Women's Welfare League, Te Pihopatanga o Aotearoa (the Maori section of the Anglican Church), Te Kohanga Reo Trust (the co-ordinating body for the Maori language nests which teach Maori to pre-schoolers) and others. Every kohanga reo in the country became a member and supporter of ABS. Significantly, the Kohanga Reo Trust, which epitomised the investment in the future of Maori language and culture, recognised the benefits and boldness of the ABS initiative and invested in it.

But still Mr Wetere was unmoved. With hindsight, it is possible to see how events then began to turn against ABS. Ian Cross was squeezed out of his position at BCNZ, and daily control of this country's public broadcasting system passed into the hands of executives from overseas with the appointment of a commercially minded Australian, Nigel Dick, as chief executive of the Broadcasting Corporation of New Zealand, and an Englishman, Julian Mounter, as head of Television New Zealand.

The arrival of these two foreigners spelled the death knell for ABS's third channel hopes. Despite the arrangement we had, the BCNZ pulled out just three weeks before the Aotearoa Broadcasting System was due to appear before the Broadcasting Tribunal, leaving us no time to make other arrangements. Mr Dick had decided to fight the third channel contenders, and used the excuse of the still-unsecured $15 million guarantee for the BCNZ's withdrawal. As a sop, Mr Dick talked to ABS about running a radio network, but in the end, the BCNZ walked away from that offer too, having found more compliant people to deal with. ABS did appear before the Tribunal and presented evidence from 59 witnesses. But it was unable to provide the financial guarantees.

ABS had gone to the hearings to talk about philosophy and fair play, and an equitable share for Maori in the country's broadcasting system. For a time it even had the financial underpinning to make it work. But the Tribunal that had drawn up the rules of the game, and the Minister who endorsed it, were in no mood to listen. As another sop to Maori, the Tribunal co-opted a Maori member, Wiremu Kerekere, a former broadcaster. He didn't have the background to be influential — and, in any case, he had no vote.

ABS lost its bid for the third channel warrants. There are those who say that it won in other ways, pointing to various developments in the public broadcasting system since then. But each of these was minimal. And progress after six decades of radio and three of television is still so slight that it's easily missed.

Television New Zealand and Radio New Zealand are now state-owned enterprises, charged with efficient commercial operation. Given how little was achieved under the publicly accountable BCNZ, what hope is there in the new environment of the state-owned enterprises?

As a footnote, I return to the Maori radio network offered by the BCNZ after it had backed out of its agreement with ABS.

The Maori Radio Board, formed to establish a Maori radio network, was set up by the BCNZ. Although called a board, in fact its only legal status was that of an advisory committee to the BCNZ. It was an amateur board with no broad-casters, to be advised by Radio New Zealand. In the publicity which surrounded the announcement of this new development, Radio New Zealand's Director-

General, Beverley Wakem, said Maori radio development would be given top priority and would be placed ahead of any other Radio New Zealand developments.

Within months, she appeared before the Board of Maori Affairs asking for funding, saying that without it, the development would founder. Amazingly, a Government which was unable to give a guarantee to ABS — remember, only a guarantee was required, not cash — now found the necessary cash for Radio New Zealand.

More than two years on, and after enjoying the highest level of public funding of any Maori broadcasting group, the Maori Radio Board has achieved little. It was not included in the restructuring of the public sector of broadcasting, but rather was pushed out of the nest, and has since turned itself into a trust — now called the Aotearoa Maori Radio Trust. The same principals have appointed themselves trustees and claim the support of Cabinet.

So far, their broadcasting prowess has been demonstrated in one six-week broadcast in Auckland. Few of the staff have experience in radio longer than that broadcast. At the time of writing, only one is a native Maori speaker. The format they lean towards is that of a pop music station catering for young people. There are already six such stations in the Auckland area. Their plan is to be bilingual by announcing records in Maori or English. And they'll be an all-Maori station one day a week, probably on Sunday.

While not necessarily an undesirable service, surely this is not the first development needed in Maori broadcasting, nor the one that should receive the lion's share of public funding. For me, the Aotearoa Broadcasting System held out the hope of an independent and autonomous Maori media outlet, something which is sorely needed in this country where every Maori initiative is affected by hostile, ill-informed and often arrogant news reporting.

That Maori media outlet needs to be designed by Maori people, not imposed by Pakeha, who have failed in the past to meet the Crown's obligations but continue to interfere, as is the case with the Maori Radio Board and Television New Zealand. The longer it takes to achieve an ABS-type development, the more race relations will deteriorate as the present Pakeha media continue to deliver messages of misinformation, intolerance and prejudice.

Chapter 20

PACIFIC ISLAND RESPONSES TO OUR MONOCULTURAL MEDIA

Samson Samasoni

We are doing well, we're not shouting about it. There are successful [Pacific Island] faces in New Zealand, faces white New Zealand won't always be able to ignore. These are the faces that will silence the generations, and yes, the racism.[1]

In April 1989, the *Sunday Star* ran an article on Pacific Island people in New Zealand which led with the above comment from one of the many young Pacific Island lawyers now practising in New Zealand. The piece was written by a Pacific Island reporter. Fifteen years ago the number of Pacific Island law graduates in this country may have just reached double figures. The number of Pacific Island journalists could have been counted on one hand.

In 1986, census statistics indicated there were 125 800 people in New Zealand who identified themselves as Pacific Islanders — that is, 3.9 percent of the population. Addressing members of this group, a respected High Court judge recently commented that 'the people of New Zealand are fed up with you coming and taking what you can get and then claiming the benefit of what you prefer to have from your own way of life'.[2]

Certainly in that particular case, the Samoan family he was directing his comments to were being sentenced for some serious offences. But more significant was how the judge was able to express his own perception of Pacific Islanders, and then through the media reinforce popular beliefs. This is how the 'system' and the media unknowingly conspire to foster negative myths and prejudices.

In 1951, there were about 3 600 Pacific Island people in New Zealand. It was not until the late 1960s and 1970s that people from the Pacific started coming here in larger numbers. The image of the uneducated, non-English-speaking Islander remains strong in the minds of many New Zealanders — too strong to be contradicted by reality.

Over 65 percent of the Pacific Island people in this country are under the age of 30, and more than three-quarters of them were actually born here. Sixty-four percent of the Pacific Island population in New Zealand live in Auckland. There are six main Pacific Island communities in New Zealand. They are: Samoan (51.3 percent of the Pacific Island population in New Zealand), Cook Island (25.5), Tongan (10.3), Niuean (9.5), Tokelauan (1.9) and Fijian (1.5). It is often forgotten that Cook Islanders, Niueans and Tokelauans qualify automatically for New Zealand citizenship, so more than one-third of the Pacific Island population here are already New Zealanders. Yet as a result of media coverage all Pacific Island people tend to be lumped together and associated in the public mind with 'over-staying' and unemployment.

Since about half of the Pacific Island population here are New Zealand born and one-third are New Zealand citizens by right, there are in fact not too many left over for anyone to get upset about. But the New Zealand media have unconsciously perpetuated the notion that Pacific Island people are a blight on society. The reason for this is simple: news editors, chief reporters, reporters and sub-editors all bring with them their personal fears and prejudices. While paying lip-service to objectivity, journalists unwittingly help to mould, shape and influence our attitudes in a variety of ways.

The media present us with material which is entertaining or newsworthy, but always in a monocultural Pakeha sense. Only recently have Pacific Island people been numbered among these influential opinion-makers.

Those who have settled here have eagerly adopted their new home, but they can still feel slighted when their contributions to this country, economically and socially, are reported unsympathetically. It has long been familiar here for media reports to refer to a convicted Pacific Island felon as a Samoan or Niuean while an All Black from the Pacific Islands is simply a New Zealander. Mercifully, most media organisations have now stopped identifying Pacific Island defendants in court cases by their ethnic origin.

Being excluded from the media is almost as disheartening as being portrayed negatively. For any group to feel truly accepted in a society, there is a need to see themselves actively involved in all aspects of that society. Some journalists argue that the media merely offer a mirror to reflect our society, but for Pacific Island people they present a window through which they view someone else's world.

Government agencies are now fully aware of their responsibilities to serve all communities in New Zealand, Pacific Island people included. Department newsletters and advertising such as television's embarrassingly successful Access Training Campaign are striving to reflect this awareness. However, private sector interests are harder to convince, since the Pacific Island population does not yet present a significant market for goods or services. Until it does, we will not see a marked increase in the number of Pacific Island people featured on television. Yet, as the Pacific Island population expands, we can expect a change in commercial targeting.

If Pacific Island people have a negative image in the general media, or are simply not represented, then one solution is to develop their own media. The monthly Wellington-based Pacific Island magazine *Pasefika* summed this up in its first editorial:

> When the Pacific Island people have rejoiced, they have celebrated without a media presence; when they are sad, it has been at the centre of the public eye.
>
> The New Zealand news media is a beast the Pacific Island people cannot relate to, cannot understand and, most of all, cannot trust.
>
> It is for these reasons that we as Pacific Island people living in New Zealand must create our own media. We must bask in the glories of our children's achievements, we must celebrate the success of our brothers and sisters, and we must come together in times of sadness and be united.

Until recently, such alternative initiatives were handicapped by a shortage of people with the required skills. The situation has now changed completely. In 1984, there were about half a dozen people of Pacific Island origin working as journalists in New Zealand. By 1989, more than 50 Pacific Islanders had been formally trained in journalism, many through the Pacific Island Journalism Course at Manukau Polytechnic, and over 300 more had either attended introductory courses or were involved with the Newspapers In Education programme in their schools.

At the time of writing, most daily metropolitan newspapers employ Pacific Island journalists. Others work on magazines or in radio and television. With the skilled people available, creating Pacific Island media is now possible. The following are some of the pioneers:

Te Kuki Airani is a Cook Island bilingual (English/Cook Island Maori) tabloid newspaper, established in 1988 by a Manukau graduate, which provides a service to an eager but, in business terms, small community. The Auckland-based publication is clearly laid out and well written, yet its experience epitomises the difficulties facing minority publications. Slim on advertising, the newspaper relies heavily on sales, but at $1.50 for a 12-page issue, it is expensive, particularly for its targeted customers.

Another tabloid attempted to solve these economic problems by catering to a larger audience. Established in 1988 on sound commercial terms and aimed at the Auckland market, the fortnightly English language *Pacific Press* felt it had a winning formula. After several months of unanticipated resistance from advertisers and poor sales, the paper was forced to close.

Pasefika took some bold steps. It ran stories in seven languages (the main Pacific Island languages and English) and was distributed free. The publisher believed that the magazine, which focused on a younger readership, had to become an accepted part of the Pacific Island community before it could be sold successfully. Again, the venture was under-capitalised and there was difficulty with advertising. At the time of writing, those involved in *Pasefika* are forming an incorporated society to operate the magazine as a community venture.

Samoana is the longest running New Zealand-based Pacific Island publication. The weekly tabloid, which has been in operation for more than seven years, is sold in New Zealand, but its main market is Samoa, where it has an office. It can also be obtained in Australia, American Samoa, Hawaii and Los Angeles.

Many local communities are also served by newsletters which circulate among smaller groups. For example, the Tokelauan community in Lower Hutt has a quarterly newsletter featuring a mix of news, information and stories or traditional songs of interest. These publications represent private or community attempts to create a more positive, balanced media, but there have also been government-funded efforts on radio and television.

National Radio's *Pacific Islands News Magazine* is still the most popular source of news for Pacific Island communities. Broadcast in the Pacific Island languages, the programme caters mainly for the older Pacific Island audience and features a magazine item from a different Island group each week night. National Radio also has *Tagata Atumotu*, a weekly 30-minute programme in English which looks at Pacific issues.

Access radio has a strong Pacific Island following because it is the people of the community themselves who make the programmes (see chapter 9). Most Pacific Island groups are represented, and in some communities access radio is replacing the newsletter as a more regular and interesting type of bulletin board. Pacific Island groups involved are fearful of the threat to access radio in a deregulated, restructured media environment.

Saturday morning's *Tagata Pasifika* is Television New Zealand's only formal Pacific Island television programme, but since it attracts little advertising money, it too is under-resourced. Pacific Island people are nonetheless having an impact on television generally. Actor Jay Laga'aia is regularly seen on television, in both programmes and advertisements. Kids' show presenters Catherine McPherson and Ole Maiava are well-known television personalities. Susan Lei'ataua has also made a contribution on both television and radio. And then, of course, Natalie Brunt is familiar to most New Zealanders.

It will certainly not be long before we see the mainstream media taking more notice of Pacific Island communities. Pacific Island people now comprise more than 10 percent of the Auckland population. Some businesses are already considering strategies to effectively target the Pacific Island market, which in future years will be of far greater commercial significance. We can look forward to Pacific Island supplements in the metropolitan dailies, and whole sections devoted to the different Pacific Island communities. There is already talk of commercial groups with major financial backing developing New Zealand-based Pacific Island publications.

The New Zealand media have generally been unkind and unfair to Pacific Island people. While many improvements have now been made, incidents such as the 1988 killing of a Tongan at the Otara Shopping Mall (see chapter 17) reveal that the media may still fall back on their prejudiced instincts.

The Pacific Island communities resident in New Zealand (which include an increasing proportion born in New Zealand) are involved with initiatives to restore a balance in public perceptions — at least within their own communities. They are developing ethnic-specific media to meet a demand for accurate information. In time, commercial imperatives will force private media interests to recognise their importance. In the meantime, New Zealand's mainstream media, with some exceptions, will continue to reinforce the racism directed at Pacific Islanders to the detriment of good race relations.

IV

DIRECTIONS

THIS FINAL SECTION offers suggestions from two experienced media people on how the media could improve its performance. James Tully provides a set of guidelines for journalists to follow when reporting on race relations. He is highly critical of the media, regarding it as a mono-cultural institution which fails to reflect the bicultural, and multi-ethnic nature of this society. Allison Webber explains how her experience has led her to consider new options and to be more conscious of the dominant values of the media, the mediatanga. She challenges journalists and the media to become bicultural.

Contributors to this book have pointed up various aspects of racism in New Zealand's media. There is a manifest need for existing values and practices in the media to be carefully and critically scrutinised. The challenge for journalists and media organisations is to show by example that it is possible to report on all events and issues of public concern in a sensitive and equitable way without compromising media principles. Indeed, a more responsible and self-critical approach could raise media standards immeasurably. More Maori and Pacific Island people are needed both as journalists and in decisionmaking roles. Viable options should be created for those minority groups who want to establish their own, independent media. Media representatives need to take responsibility for these changes, for if there is no change, the implications for our future race relations are serious.

Chapter 21

A CODE OF ETHICS FOR JOURNALISTS REPORTING ON RACE RELATIONS

James Tully

The role of the news media in reporting race relations in New Zealand has not escaped critical evaluation in the past. Most negative comment has been directed at specific examples of what the critics see as inadequate, sensational or just plain bad reporting.

There have also been the predictable sweeping attacks on the news media as a white male system unable, if not unwilling, to report competently Maori aspirations and concerns and what is loosely called Maori news. This is seen as the result of rigid criteria for newsworthiness and story construction and an inherent racism.

True enough, there have been some notable examples of insensitive and/or incompetent reporting, but the general attacks on the news media present a distorted picture that does not fairly reflect the steady stream of excellent reporting on Maori and Pacific Island people, events and issues. I was a judge in the print section of the Media Peace Awards and found it heartening to read culturally sensitive, thoughtful and challenging feature articles in newspapers, magazines and special interest publications.

I believe most journalists want to improve the standard of race relations reporting and coverage of things Polynesian. Most want to see New Zealand work through our present tensions to a climate of resolution and accept that the news media have a key role as a forum for the challenging discussions that must take place over how true biculturalism and partnership consistent with the spirit of the Treaty of Waitangi can be achieved.

Some argue that the news media should consciously work to improve race relations because of the strong correlation between race relations reporting and racial attitudes among the public. The way in which the news media portray Maori and Pacific Islanders and race relations issues has a significant impact on how New Zealanders perceive these aspects of life: whether there is tolerance or prejudice, understanding or hostility. The news media can do much good or harm, and cannot escape a central role in race relations.

Generally, reporters and editors have made their own rules for handling race relations and reporting Maori affairs based on traditional attitudes to the role of the media, newsworthiness and media ethics. It has become increasingly obvious that these traditional values and methods must be reviewed and in many cases overhauled in light of the changing needs and expectations of the audience (readers, viewers, listeners), improved education, technological advances and the increasing complexity of modern society.

The role of the news media in race relations is clear: to inform, to educate and to explain. New Zealanders must know what is happening and what is being said even if the message is unpalatable and likely to inflame passions. Coming to terms with multiculturalism won't be achieved by suppressing some views and presenting a distorted picture.

The news media must also work hard at educating the public so the issues are fully understood and extreme views put into perspective. The options for the future must be spelt out. If most New Zealanders have not grasped what is meant by partnership or power-sharing, then the news media have failed in an important duty.

However, it is not enough to define the issues and simply tell it as it is. Journalists must explain the changes taking place in society, with reference to, and an understanding of, the past as well as identifying and interpreting contemporary trends and developments.

The criteria for newsworthiness which reflect a British–North American tradition need to be reviewed. Those which are no longer appropriate should be modified or rejected.

The emphasis on timeliness is understandable when news organisations are competing to be 'first with the news' and put a premium on immediacy, relevance and topicality. But a great deal of news is rejected because it is difficult to determine the time-frame of a trend or process. There is a vital need to explain the underlying causes of social problems, and what it is like to be a Maori or Pacific Islander in New Zealand.

The journalism textbooks also uphold public prominence (how important a person is) as a key factor in story selection. Once again, there is a logical basis for this approach, but what of the so-called 'invisible people' and those whose importance is based on achievements or a standing in the community that do not fit neatly into the usual criteria for prominence? We publish obituaries of borough councillors but often overlook a local kaumatua.

The reactive, event-oriented nature of so much New Zealand journalism conditions readers, listeners and viewers to see the news as a series of crises which generally embody conflict, the element of news selection that takes priority. The impression is of a state of tension and confrontation that does not accurately reflect the world as most of us know and experience it. By focusing on crises and conflict, the public is led to believe race relations are deteriorating or are more highly charged than they actually are. Our worst fears and prejudices are confirmed by stories that highlight conflict.

Two-dimensional debates which focus on polarised views make good copy but do little to create a climate of resolution. If the news media focus on 'extremists' and continually play up polarised views, race relations must suffer. The unpalatable must be reported but it must be kept in perspective and balanced by the very positive things that are happening, albeit in a low-key, even mundane way that does not fit traditional criteria for newsworthiness.

In reviewing the news selection process, the relationship between journalists and their sources must not be ignored. The range of sources tends to be relatively narrow, with reporters generally dealing with official spokespeople who are accessible and available. Of course, you don't have to be an official talking head if you say something extreme or sensational enough. This is the stuff of which overnight personalities are made.

The reporter who seeks to adequately report Maori and Pacific Island communities (or indeed the invisible people of our society as a whole) must develop a much wider range of sources and relate to them in a way which recognises cultural differences. For their part, editors must be prepared to run stories that may not fit neatly into existing patterns of news selection.

This review of traditional attitudes should extend to the concept of objectivity. Many reporters, in my experience, believe objectivity is both possible and desirable. They have been conditioned to be objective and assume that if a report is accurate and fair and balanced, objectivity has been achieved. But absolute objectivity is unattainable. Every journalist operates with certain assumptions and values — beliefs about nation and society, and assumptions about what constitutes 'normal behaviour'. The American journalist Walter Lippman put it this way: 'The facts we see depend on where we are placed and the habits of our eyes.' And distinguished British editor Harold Evans wrote: 'Facts may be sacred, but which facts?' Exactly. We select what we mirror; we allocate the time and space devoted to an item; we determine how it will be presented.

Journalists are storytellers, transmitting information from source to audience — summarising, refining and altering that information to make it suitable for their audience. So objectivity means, at best, a general striving towards a neutral, detached and value-free approach.

Real objectivity, says Evans, requires a positive commitment. When a news source distorts the truth, the reporter has a responsibility to include in the story the most reliable information obtainable. 'So long as it is clear what is fact and what is interpretation we have a duty to keep the record straight.' This conception of objectivity is rather different from that which many New Zealand journalists accept. It is, however, an essential starting point if our news media are to play a truly positive role in improving race relations.

Some basic working principles of good journalism for reporting and commenting on racial and communal issues are desirable. Media ethics have been rightly described as a 'slippery topic' at the junction of theory and practice. For many journalists it's a case of 'I know it when I see it' — situational ethics with decisions shaped by urgency and intuition where there should be deliberation and finely drawn distinctions.

There are few absolutes in media ethics. Editorial styles and priorities, audiences, tone and taste can vary widely. However, I believe the following principles, adapted from principles evolved at a recent Press Foundation of Asia seminar, provide a set of ethical guidelines all responsible journalists could accept:

- Avoid stereotypes and generalisation. They fuel prejudice and keep superficial the level of debate and analysis.
- Avoid slogans and labels. Terms such as 'activist' and 'moderate' are easily

applied, but are not particularly helpful. They also reinforce prejudices; indeed, they can undermine the credibility of individuals and groups and cause people to ignore what's being said. The term 'activist', for example, is generally the kiss of death to someone's credibility in New Zealand.

- Avoid race-typing and irrelevant references to people's colour or race.
- Take care with statistics. They should always be checked, interpreted and put in context.
- Take particular care with headlines. In the pressure to write a strong attention-grabbing heading, don't use language that will excite passions. Headings and lead paragraphs must always be justified by the story.
- Be careful with pictures and film not representative of an event or incident.
- Carefully evaluate the authority of sources, especially when their comments, allegations or criticisms are likely to increase tension. And always name sources unless non-attribution is absolutely necessary.
- Don't publish unverified rumour. Contradiction should be specific. It is generally irresponsible to predict violence.
- Make every effort to portray positive aspects of race relations and multi-culturalism.
- Don't exploit human fears for commercial gain.

Chapter 22

THE NEED FOR CHANGE: RESPONSIBILITIES OF THE MEDIA

Allison Webber

Being confronted by my own mediatanga has been one of the most painful and rewarding experiences of the last 10 years. I can still remember an occasion, back in 1983, when I met with a group of what we in the media would label 'Maori radicals' to talk about a proposed television series on racism.

Yes, I'd be happy to help them make the series but I didn't really have time, I said. But it's your problem, your responsibility, they said. No it's not, because you're the people most affected by it, I said. But you have the power and it's that power that screws us up, they said. Suddenly the penny dropped, and in a flash I knew what was meant by institutional racism. What's more I knew that I was part of it.

Even though being challenged in a fairly heavy way isn't exactly one of the fun parts of the job, it was and still is very necessary. I know that if I hadn't been challenged I wouldn't have received the mental kick in the head I needed to make me change. From then on began a journey.

In starting this journey I had to acknowledge that in the first half of my career, I had hardly ever interviewed a Maori, that most of the research skills I used were inappropriate in the Maori world. I had to acknowledge that while I had travelled to South Africa and championed the anti-apartheid cause, there were direct similarities here. No, we didn't have a racist system as severely entrenched in the law, but we as Pakeha had set the agenda. It was our table the Maori were being asked to dine at and our knives and forks they were being asked to use.

It was not easy acknowledging that I had almost no knowledge of Maori issues, history or protocol; that I had never been on a marae, and had almost no understanding of the language. What was even more difficult was to be told loud and clear that Maori were running out of patience with this kind of wimpish impotence. They had more than enough to do raising their own status from rock bottom. On top of this, educating the Pakeha in things we had chosen to ignore for the past 150 years was not a top priority.

So, what to do about it? It is my belief that we have to change. Firstly, because I believe we have obligations under the Treaty to do so; secondly, because we don't deserve to call ourselves 'the media' or 'the press' if we don't do so; and thirdly, because it makes sound economic sense to cater for the 15 percent or more of the population who haven't properly been heard from.

The changes I think we need to make are first of all at a personal level. We need to look at the values and the processes we employ in the media. We need to unpick them and put them back together in a new shape. Most importantly, we need to recognise that the debate going on 'out there' about the Treaty is not just something we need to cover fully — it concerns us: how we work, how we run our newsrooms, what we publish/broadcast, who we employ and train and the stereotypes we reinforce.

This means a fundamental assault on that most prized piece of journalistic armour — objectivity. For years, we've hidden behind its shield, and this has always given us a great excuse to ignore our own processes and prejudices. If one is driven by a belief in unfaltering objectivity, then there is no need to debate one's values and their impact on the wider public.

Recently I've come to see that my objectivity involves a highly subjective set of Pakeha values handed down to me over the past 20 years. They're to do with the very idea of what actually constitutes news. I've come to see that one of the greatest myths of our age is that the daily news is actually 'The News'. In reality, 'news' is a catalogue of daily events and incidents selected using a prescribed set of values handed down to us from our great media colonisers, the Americans and the British. They set the agenda of what was, and still is, newsworthy, and to a large degree we've followed it. This is part of our mediatanga — our media culture.

It's ironic that while many sections of our society, from health and education through to the environmental and trade union movements, have been analysing their structures and debating their equity, we in the media have covered these debates, but have failed to see the relevance to ourselves — our own structures, our own values. This lack of debate and analysis has often left us in a reactionary position, capable of undermining the many enlightened and costly initiatives set up to increase racial understanding in the wider community.

Having looked at our own culture and values, I believe we then need to apply a form of bicultural audit to what we do. This kind of auditing procedure is standard journalistic practice with legal matters. We look at our stories from all angles to check whether they are potentially defamatory. In the same way, we could look at them to see if they've really told the full story from a Maori and a Pakeha point of view. Were there Maori we could have asked for comment but didn't? Were the questions we asked biased? Did the story reinforce stereotypes or increase understanding? Was the process of writing and gathering the news culturally sensitive?

Education at all levels must go hand in hand with any changes. While it is pleasing that there are moves afoot to introduce a bicultural programme as part of the core curriculum in pre-entry journalism courses, this is just the tip of the iceberg. There is little point in training a new generation of journalists to work biculturally when they are blocked from using these practices in the workplace.

The current education programme hasn't entirely achieved its stated aims. TVNZ's Kimihia programme has gone some way to setting clear goals for employment and for change. Allied to the programme was the requirement for bicultural training to be carried out at all levels of management. This used a top-down approach and has worked its way down through various levels of management. It's this kind of commitment to education and change that's needed in other branches of the media.

We need to set a goal to work towards, such as truly bicultural media by the year 2000 — ideally much earlier. This would mean the bicultural training of all journalists. It would also mean setting some other goals — such as the employment of 20 percent Maori and Pacific Island journalists over the next decade.

If we take as a fundamental premise that what is news depends on who gathers it and how it is gathered, then Maori and Pacific Island reporters will make a difference. Already there are a number of examples where a proactive Maori reporter has made both a qualitative and a quantitative difference to the perception of Maori issues in the community.

Philip Whaanga, from Radio New Zealand's *Checkpoint*, is one example. He has significantly lifted the profile of Maori stories, which are no longer marginalised, strong Maori stories running almost every other night. These stories also bring another model of Maoridom — one which is positive. The programmes present Maori leaders as having pertinent opinions on business, development and the economy — a far cry from the victim/bottom-of-the-heap coverage we have become used to.

While the achievements of reporters such as Philip Whaanga, Debbie Gee and Vern Rice are impressive, the experiences of these lone warriors battling with the dominant values of the Pakeha can be pretty daunting. They are expected to answer for the sins and omissions of all Maori, past and present; to be as good if not better than their Pakeha colleagues; to resolve Pakeha anxiety and ignorance about things Maori; and to answer to their own people for the daily devastation the media visit upon them. On top of this are constant assaults on the way their language is spoken and written, and the continual portrayal of their people as victims, bludgers, no-hopers and perpetrators of violence by their peers.

Another challenge is to accept that Maori events rarely fit into a Pakeha time and values framework. How do you explain to the chief reporter, who wants the story now, that the hui or the tangi might go on for three days? How do you explain that the process of making a decision is as important as the decision itself, or that what is new is not nearly as important as what has gone before? And how do you explain that while it may be the Pakeha style to use the media as a tool for resolving conflict, this is not necessarily the style of the Maori?

If we are to employ more Maori journalists in newsrooms up and down the country, we need to look at how these places operate. Because they've been run in a certain way for years and years, there's no reason why they wouldn't benefit from an overhaul which might incorporate Maori values into the existing structures.

We should also be moving towards a time when we reward biculturalism in our pay structures. Already we have a number of Maori journalists fluent in both languages, but there is no reward for this when the pay cheques come in each week. These journalists are more skilled and more useful than their colleagues who only speak one language. If we pay a margin for skill to reporters who write high speed shorthand, there seems no reason why bilingual fluency shouldn't be equally rewarded. After all, there are many important events where an English-only reporter would be totally inept, and have less competence than a five-year-old kohanga reo graduate.

Finally, and most important, is the acceptance that what is news depends very much on how we gather it — that is, process. A simple example of this is the rounds system. This system provides a way by which we divide up the community and then assign reporters to 'cover' different sections of it. The rounds are usually rated hierarchically, and those at the top of the hierarchy are usually politics, the economy and business, sport, and accidents and emergencies. We get a lot of news in these areas because we work very hard to get it.

For example, let's consider the process of covering the police, accident and emergency round. We get a lot of news about crime because we believe it is important — it sells papers and therefore we work very hard to get it. Most newspapers and radio stations up and down the country will telephone the police, fire and ambulance several times a day to find out what is going on. Reporters will also make daily personal calls to the police. Many, especially on the larger papers, have police radios installed in their offices so they can monitor these activities 24 hours a day. It's hardly surprising then that we get so many stories about crime and violence.

Now, if we take this method of gathering news and compare it with the way we gather stories on the Maori world, we would find very few parallels. The Maori round is usually held in low regard, with little status in the newsgathering hierarchy, except when there is a scandal like the Maori loans or Whare Paia affairs. On such occasions, the big boys of the newsroom usually barge into the limelight. The result, frequently, is yet another round of Maori-bashing.

If we worked a fraction as hard to get Maori news as we do to fill our crime and violence quota, the whole national image of the Maori world would change dramatically. For example, the Tainui people have over 30 listed hui in their region every year, a vast majority of them totally unreported.

So, what of the future? Well, to start with, we should see it as a challenge, rather than a problem. The media in 1990 have two choices — they can take refuge in the safe confines of their presumed 'objectivity', or they can take a long-overdue look at themselves and their contribution to racism and a violent society. My hope is that we will put aside our masks of comfortable anonymity, and be prepared to examine our performance and our processes. Many other groups in our society have travelled this path.

By the turn of the century, one in every two school-leavers north of Taupo will be Maori, and half of them will probably have no job. Their future, and their sense of belonging, is at stake.

In this period of change, the media have a clear role and challenge — to ensure that the voices of all in this country are heard. There is much to be shared. Perhaps all we in the media need to learn is the skill of listening. It could be a revolutionary experience.

Notes and References

Chapter 1
1. Farnsworth, 1984: 56.
2. *New Zealand Official Yearbook*, 1987.
3. Hall, 1977.
4. Misa, 1987: 57.
5. Lewis and Pearlman, 1986.
6. Downes and Harcourt, 1976: 151.
7. Klapper, 1960.
8. Lewis and Pearlman, 1986: 147.
9. Lewis and Pearlman, 1986.
10. This example is adapted from L. Masterman, 1986.
11. Hall, 1986.
12. Loader and Bosshard, 1987.
13. Robin Kora, newsreader for *Eyewitness News*, was removed after controversy about his reading style.
14. Thompson, 1984: 4.
15. MacRae, 1986/7: 34–6.
16. Cleveland, 1971.
17. Fox, 1988.
18. Fox, 1988.
19. This section is based on Ericson et al., 1987.
20. Morley, 1980.
21. Farnsworth, 1988: 469.
22. Fox, 1988.
23. Golding and Murdoch, 1986: 175–94.

Chapter 2
1. Husband, 1975: 28.
2. Kelsey, 1988.
3. Kelsey, 1988: 5.
4. Verma, 1988: 123.
5. Matabane, 1988.
6. Matabane, 1988: 30.
7. The Race Relations Conciliator's report of 1986 commented in relation to public statements by a Minister of Immigration of the mid-1970s, the Hon T. F. Gill: 'The underlying premise of the Minister's statement is that immigration is a threat which must be controlled; his equation of overstaying with disease is both revealing and irrational. . . . We submit that the racism involved in stereotyping and targeting Pacific Islander groups during the overstayer campaigns of 1974–76 has remained an influence in the Department [of Immigration].'
8. Race Relations Conciliator, 1986.
9. Spoonley, 1988.
10. Allan (*Metro*, March 1988) questions press coverage of the so-called migration to Australia, and notably Queensland, and suggests that the *New Zealand Herald* has 'invented a wave of mass migration' which is not supported by the facts.
11. Murupaenga, 1988.
12. Ford, 1988: 38.
13. Lealand, 1988.
14. Cave, 1986.
15. Joshua, Wallace and Booth, 1973.
16. Fife, 1987.
17. Cross, 1988.
18. Evans, 1976: 9.
19. Parekh, 1988.

Chapter 3
1. For further discussion, see chapter 16.
2. For further discussion, see chapter 14.

Chapter 4
1. Finding of the Waitangi Tribunal Relating to Te Reo Maori and a Claim Lodged by Huirangi Waikerepuru and Nga Kaiwhakapumau i te Reo Incorporated Society, Wellington 1986.
2. Lealand, Wellington 1988.
3. Tremewan, 1986/87.

Chapter 5
1. Thompson, 1955: 33–4.
2. Dansey, 1977: 12.
3. New Zealand Press Council, 'Racial References in Crime Reports', Guidance Note, privately circulated, 30 June 1986.
4. Ibid.

Chapter 6.
1. National Economic Research Associates, *Management of the Radio Frequency Spectrum in New Zealand*, Wellington 1989.

Chapter 7
1. *Auckland Star*, 22 September 1988.
2. Christchurch *Press*, 10 January 1989.
3. *Dominion Sunday Times*, 4 September 1988.
4. Smith, 1987.
5. Lichter et al., 1987.
6. Ibid.
7. Ibid.
8. Ibid.
9. *Televiews 10*, 14 March 1988.
10. Fiske, 1987: 320.
11. *Dominion Sunday Times*, 22 January 1989.

Chapter 11
1. Examples include: Challenger, N., 'Outlook: Sharing Links with the Land' (8/11/88); Habib, G., 'Right to Fish as Ancient as Maui' (2/9/88); Temm, P., 'Treaty Past, Treaty Present' (13/8/88).

Chapter 12
1. *Kompas*, 23 September 1987 (Indonesia).
2. *The West Australian*, 1 March 1989.
3. *The Globe and Mail*, Canada, 18 March 1989.

4. *The Age*, Melbourne, 4 February 1989.
5. *Kompas*, 23 September 1987.
6. *Indonesian Times*, 24 July 1987. The capitalised words appear in the original.
7. *Kompas*, 23 September 1987.
8. Ibid.
9. *Le Figaro*, 4 April 1987.
10. *Le Monde*, 12 January 1989.
11. *Asahi Shimbun Weekly*, 14 February 1989.
12. *Financial Times*, 20 July 1988.
13. *New York Times*, 14 February 1988.
14. *The Bulletin*, 31 May 1988.
15. *Penthouse* (Australia), December 1988.
16. *Penthouse* (Australia), January 1989.
17. *Sydney Morning Herald*, 19 April 1988.
18. *Penthouse* (Australia), December 1988.
19. Ibid.
20. *The Bulletin*, 23 August 1988.
21. *Canberra Times*, 17 May 1989.
22. *The Bulletin*, 23 August 1988.
23. Ibid.
24. *Canberra Times*, 28 January 1989.
25. *Penthouse* (Australia), January 1989.
26. *Financial Review*, 13 October 1988.

Chapter 15
1. Case file A359, Race Relations Office.
2. De Bres, *New Zealand Monthly Review*, May 1976.
3. *Auckland Star*, 22 October 1976.

Chapter 17
1. *Auckland Star*, 28 October 1988.
2. *Auckland Star*, 11 August 1988.
3. *Auckland Star*, 4 May 1989.

Chapter 20
1. *Sunday Star*, April 1989.
2. *Auckland Star*, 19 June 1989.

Select Bibliography

Allan, J. 'How the Herald Invented a Wave of Mass Migration.' *Metro*, March 1988.

Asare, K. L. 'Two Channels or Three? An Exploration of Viewers' Opinions.' A master of business studies research report. Massey University, 1986.

Atkin, C. K., Greenberg, B. S., and McDermott, S. 'Television and Race Role Socialisation.' *Journalism Quarterly* 60: 3, Autumn 1983.

Belich, J. *The New Zealand Wars*. Auckland 1986.

Bonney, B., and Wilson, H. *Australia's Commercial Media*. Sydney 1983.

Cave, S. 'Maori Radio: Autonomy on the Air?' *Listener*, 8 November 1986.

Cleveland, L. 'The NZPA and the Newspaper System.' *Political Science* 25: 32, 1971.

Cohen, P., and Gardner, C. *It Ain't Half Racist, Mum: Fighting Racism in the Media*. London 1982.

Cross, I. 'Journalists Must Decamp from Olympus.' *Evening Post*, 9 December 1988.

Dansey, H. D. B. Report of the Race Relations Conciliator for the Year Ending 31 March 1977, Wellington 1977.

Downes, P., and Harcourt, P. *Voices in the Air: Radio Broadcasting in New Zealand — A Documentary*. Wellington 1976.

Ericson, R., Baranek, P., and Chan, J. *Visualising Deviance: A Study of News Organisation*. Milton Keynes 1987.

Evans, P. *Publish and Be Damned?* London 1976.

Farnsworth, J. 'Media Studies in New Zealand.' *Sites: A Journal for Radical Perspectives on Culture*, Issue 9, 1984.

——————— 'Social Policy and Media in New Zealand.' Royal Commission on Social Policy. *Social Perspectives*, Vol. 4: 457–480, Wellington 1988.

Fife, M. 'Promoting Racial Diversity in U.S. Broadcasting: Federal Policies versus Social Realities.' *Media, Culture and Society* 9: 481–504, 1987.

Fiske, J. *Television Culture*. London 1987.

Ford, G. 'Newsmakers.' *Listener*, 10 December 1988.

Fox, D. T. 'The Mass Media: A Maori Perspective.' Royal Commission on Social Policy. *Social Perspectives*, Vol. 4: 483–503, Wellington 1988.

Golding, P., and Murdoch, G. 'The New Communications Revolution.' In J. Curran et al. (eds) *Bending Reality: The State of the Media*. London 1986.

Hall, S. 'Culture, the Media and the Ideological Effect.' In J. Curran et al. (eds) *Mass Communication and Society*. London 1977.

——————— 'Media Power and Class Power.' In J. Curran et al. (eds) *Bending Reality: The State of the Media*. London 1986.

Husband, C. 'Racism in Society and the Mass Media: A Critical Interaction.' In C. Husband (ed.) *White Media and Black Britain*. London 1975.

Jesson, B., Ryan, A., and Spoonley, P. *Revival of the Right: New Zealand Politics in the 1980s*. Auckland 1988.

Johnson, P. *A History of the Jews*. London 1987.

Joshua, H., Wallace, T., and Booth, H. *To Ride the Storm: The 1980 Bristol Riot and the State*. London 1983.

Kawharu, I. H. *Maori Land Tenure*. Oxford 1977.

Kelsey, J. 'Free Market "Rogernomics" and Maori Rights under the Treaty of Waitangi — An Irresolvable Contradiction.' Paper presented to the Australian Law and Society Conference, Melbourne 1988.

Klapper, T. *The Effects of Mass Communication*. New York 1960.

Lealand, G. 'National Survey of New Zealand Journalists.' New Zealand Council for Educational Research and New Zealand Journalists' Training Board. Wellington 1988.

———————— 'Young, Trained and Female: A National Survey of New Zealand Journalists.' Paper presented to Oz Media '88 Conference, Queensland Institute of Technology, September 1988.

Lewis, P., and Pearlman, C. *Media and Power: From Marconi to Murdoch*. London 1986.

Lichter, S. R., et al. 'Prime-time Prejudice: TV's Images of Blacks and Hispanics.' *Public Opinion*, July–August 1987.

Loader, S., and Bosshard, A. 'Surrendering Our Consciences: TV News and Current Affairs.' *Illusions* 5: 30–36, 1987.

MacRae, T. 'Two Men, Two Different Paths.' *Tu Tangata*, Issue 33, 1986/87.

Masterman, L. *Learning the Media*. London 1986.

Matabane, P. W. 'Television and the Black Audience: Cultivating Moderate Perspectives on Racial Integration.' *Journal of Communication*, 38(4): 21–31, 1988.

Miller, H. *Race Conflict in New Zealand*. Auckland 1966.

Misa, T. 'All the Politician's Men: How the Ad Agencies and Strategists Conspire to Capture Your Vote.' *North and South*, August 1987.

Morley, D. *The Nationwide Audience*. London 1980.

Murupaenga, J. 'Kill a White: What Really Happened.' *Metro*, September 1988.

Orange, C. *The Treaty of Waitangi*. Wellington 1987.

Parekh, B. 'Prejudice and the Press.' *New Society*, 7 November 1988.

Prager, D., and Telushkin, J. *Why the Jews? The Reason for Anti-Semitism*. New York 1983.

Race Relations Conciliator. 'Investigation into Allegations of Discrimination in the Application of Immigration Laws in New Zealand.' Office of the Race Relations Conciliator, Auckland 1986.

Ross, R. 'The Treaty on the Ground.' In *The Treaty of Waitangi: Its Origins and Significance*. Wellington 1972.

Smith, R. 'Race and Society.' *New Society*, 2 October 1987.

Spoonley, P. *Racism and Ethnicity*. Auckland 1988.

———————— *The Politics of Nostalgia: Racism and the Extreme Right in New Zealand*. Palmerston North 1987.

Thompson, J. *Studies in the Theory of Ideology*. Cambridge 1984.

Thompson, R. H. T. 'Maori Affairs and the New Zealand Press' (Parts 1–4). *Journal of the Polynesian Society*, 62: 366–83; 63: 1–16; 64: 22–34, 1953–55.

Tremewan, P. *Tu Tangata* 33, December 1986–January 1987.

Twitchin, J. (ed.). *The Black and White Media Book. Handbook for the Study of Racism and Television*. Stoke-on-Trent 1988.

Varis, T. *International Inventory of Television Program Structure and the Flow of TV Programs Between Nations*. University of Tampere, Finland 1973.

Walker, R. J. 'The Genesis of Maori Activism.' *Journal of the Polynesian Society*, 93(3), 1984.

———————— 'The Maori People: Their Political Development.' In H. Gold, *New Zealand Politics in Perspective*. Auckland 1985.

Wall, C. 'Te Pakeha. The Search for White Identity.' *Metro*, November 1986.

Ward, A. *A Show of Justice*. Auckland 1973.

Notes on the Contributors

Gordon Campbell was born in Wanganui and has been a staff writer for the *Listener* since 1978. He tends to agree with David Halberstam when he said that in a corrupt world, the 'objective' journalist is a corrupt journalist.

Derek Fox, who is of Ngati Porou and Rongomaiwahine/Rakaipaka descent, was born in Wairoa in 1947 and grew up first with his grandparents in the Mahia area and later with his parents at Ruatoria. He has spent 20 years working in the New Zealand media, most of it in the public broadcasting system. In 1986 he terminated his contract with Television New Zealand and returned to live at Mahia from where he now undertakes freelance and consulting work in the media and related areas.

Walter Hirsh has spent 30 years in education in a diverse array of positions. He has served on many advisory committees to the Government and other organisations, and was the recipient of a Fulbright Fellowship which allowed him to study the education of ethnic minorities. He has written extensively on education, human rights and race relations, and has recently edited two books on ethnicity and equity in education. Between 1980 and 1985, he was chairperson of the New Zealand Jewish Council. He held the position of Race Relations Conciliator and Human Rights Commissioner from 1985 to 1989.

Bernard Kernot graduated in anthropology at the University of Auckland in 1963, and then taught at Ngata Memorial College at Ruatoria (1963–66), before becoming a lecturer in anthropology at Victoria University of Wellington in 1967. He is currently a senior lecturer in Maori studies. Author of *People of the Four Winds* and various articles on Maori politics and art, he is also a member of the National Justice Committee of the Catholic Commission for Justice, Peace and Development.

Stephenie Knight has an MA (Hons) in social anthropology from the University of Auckland. She has worked as a social worker, child-carer, counsellor, researcher, union delegate and university tutor. She was a founder in 1982 of Supportline for Abused Women, and has been actively involved in various areas of women's rights and social justice. She is currently Education and Research Advisor with the Race Relations Office.

Finau 'Ofa Kolo is Tongan, and has an MA (Hons) in social anthropology from the University of Auckland (1985). He was an assistant lecturer at the university during 1984 and 1985. He is currently working as an Investigating Officer with the Race Relations Office, and is an executive member of the Tonga Council.

Geoff Lealand was born in Taranaki and was educated there and at the University of Canterbury and Bowling Green State University (Ohio). He currently works with the New Zealand Council for Educational Research. He is particularly interested in media research and the study of popular culture. He was the author of *A Foreign Egg in Our Nest? American Popular Culture in New Zealand* (1988).

Steve Maharey is a senior lecturer in sociology at Massey University. He teaches media studies and is a regular commentator on the media. He is a board member of *Sites: A Journal for Radical Perspectives on Culture.*

Lesley Max was born in Auckland in 1945 and educated at Takapuna Grammar and the University of Auckland where she obtained an MA (Hons) in 1967. She taught at a comprehensive school in London. Lesley is a freelance journalist who writes for *Metro* and was a contributor to *Mental Retardation in New Zealand.* She is currently completing a book on children in New Zealand for Penguin. She is secretary of the Auckland Jewish Council and has a longstanding interest in race relations. She is married with four children.

Tipene O'Regan is the principal of Aoraki Consultant Services (Wellington), was founding chairperson of the Mawhera Incorporation and has been chairperson of the Ngai Tahu Maori Trust Board since 1983. He is a director of several companies including TVNZ Ltd and Maori International Ltd. Tipene retired in 1984 from a long-serving position as senior lecturer and head of Maori studies at Wellington Teachers College. He is a well-known writer and commentator on Maori and race relations issues. Since 1987, he has played a major role in negotiations with the Crown over Treaty issues and Maori fishing rights.

Vern Rice is from Te Arawa. He grew up in Tauranga and was educated there and in Christchurch where he completed an arts degree in Maori. He has been a daily newspaper journalist for the last five years for the *New Zealand Herald* and the *Dominion,* covering both Maori affairs and general news.

Samson Samasoni trained at Wellington Polytechnic and then became a journalist with the *Evening Post.* He is presently Secretary to the Pacific Island Employment Development Board which administers a government-funded employment scheme.

Mark Scott has worked as a dustman, fireman and thatcher and has travelled through Africa, Asia and Europe before entering journalism at the *New Zealand Herald* in 1979. He left in 1981 to start a plumbing business and to work as a freelance writer and photographer, chiefly for the *Listener.* He wrote and published *Street Action Aotearoa* (1984), a book where Maori and other Polynesian young tell of the cultural challenges they face. Born in 1956, he lives in Auckland with two daughters, Malia and Zinzi.

Paul Spoonley was brought up in Hawkes Bay and has studied at New Zealand and British universities. He has researched and written about both the New Right and Far Right in New Zealand, Australia and Britain, and about race relations in New Zealand. He has written or co-edited six books, including *Racism and Ethnicity* (1988) and *Revival of the Right: New Zealand Politics in the 1980s* (1988). He is presently a senior lecturer in sociology at Massey University. He is married with one child.

Prue Toft is currently an advisory officer with the Race Relations Office. She has an MA in anthropology which was concerned with contemporary Maori economic development. She has taught in multi-ethnic schools and has worked as an assistant lecturer in anthropology at the University of Auckland.

CONTRIBUTORS

Peter Tohill is executive director of the Race Relations Office, a position he has held for the past five years. He has been responsible for the Office's involvement in the promotion of ethnic broadcasting. He has worked with community groups to establish access community radio in Auckland. He is also chairperson of Access Radio Auckland Inc.

Andrew D. Trlin is a reader in the Department of Sociology, Massey University. His research interests include international migration and intergroup relations in Australasia, and aspects of New Zealand's social demography. He is the author of *Now Respected, Once Despised: Yugoslavs in New Zealand* (1979), co-editor with P. Spoonley of *New Zealand and International Migration: A Digest and Bibliography* (1986) and numerous other articles.

James Tully has an MA (Hons) and a Diploma in Journalism. He is director of the Graduate School of Journalism, University of Canterbury, editor of the *New Zealand Journalism Review* and president of the Journalism Tutors' Association. He was first winner of the New Zealand Journalist of the Year award (1978). He is currently researching his Ph.D. on the newspaper industry since 1945.

Ranginui J. Walker is associate professor of Maori studies at the University of Auckland. He is a member of the New Zealand Maori Council, columnist for the *Listener*, and has published many articles on Maori education, politics and activism.

Allison Webber is director of the Wellington Polytechnic Journalism School. She is a former convenor of Media Women and for the past 10 years has been committed to improving the images of women presented in the media. She has worked in the media for over 20 years as a print journalist, television researcher and producer, and as a media teacher.

Philip Whaanga is of Rakai Paaka, Ngati Kahungunu and County Kerry descent. He has been a busker, mobile librarian, photographer, radio journalist, magazine editor and fundraiser. He is currently a director of a media consultancy company, Mana Maori Media. His most satisfying job has been, with his wife Anne, parenting five children 'who'll share their bicultural heritage with other New Zealanders on firmer ground than our generation'.

Gary Wilson grew up on a farm in Helvetia, near Pukekohe, to which he has now returned. He was educated at Pukekohe Primary, King's College, the University of Auckland (BA), the University of Sydney (DipEd) and the University of California at Berkeley. He has been a teacher at St Stephen's School, Auckland, and in Toronto, a journalist (*Auckland Star* and *New Zealand Herald*), journalism tutor (ATI) and training officer (New Zealand Journalists' Training Board). He is currently a media consultant.

Overstayers
Policy
'No Con Job'

Maoris
lay clair
to 70pc
countr

Decision 'reward'
for overstayers

Rodger happy with
low overstayer haul

'Tormente
wants to quit

Overstayers Shun Permits

Kumaras
Spark
Lange
Spat

WHITE FLIG

The new class problem for our sc

Maori threat to reforms

R

M

AUDIT
CHIEFS IN
MARAE SWOOP